READY SET CONNECT

READY
SET
CONNECT

A SENSORY-BASED APPROACH TO ACCELERATE COMMUNICATION IN AUTISTIC CHILDREN

JESSIE GINSBURG, MS, CCC–SLP

FIRST EDITION

READY SET CONNECT

A Sensory-Based Approach to Accelerate
Communication in Autistic Children

Printed in the United States of America

First Edition

ISBN 979-8-218-40231-0 paperback
ISBN 979-8-218-40232-7 ebook
Library of Congress Control Number: 2024901351

Cover and Interior Design by:
Chris Treccani

Created with the Book to Millions® Method

CONTENTS

BOOK BONUSES

As a thank you for purchasing this book, I have created bonuses for you, including the Ready Set Connect Guidebook to use as you move through the book, and a free training to take advantage of at any time. Visit readysetconnectbook.com to grab your bonuses.

Download the Free Audiobook

Use this QR code or visit readysetconnectbook.com to download the free audiobook that I narrated.

Disclaimer

This book is not intended to provide medical advice and should not be used as a substitute for professional consultations or therapy. The insights and strategies shared in this book are intended to enrich discussions with families and teams, and to enhance your skills and ability to support children.

Please note that names of children and clinics have been changed to protect the privacy of families and therapists.

About the Language Used in this Book

Throughout this book, you'll see that I am using identity first language (e.g., Autistic child rather than child with autism). I default to identity first language because it's preferred by the majority of the Autistic community. Please note that just because it's preferred by most of the Autistic community (the community members who have voted through surveys), this does not mean that it's preferred by every person. Although it's safe to default to identity first language, we should always take personal preferences into consideration. You will find more information on identity first language in Chapter 8.

DEDICATION PAGE

To my favorite boys: Connor, Tucker, Jack, & Teddy

I hope you find something you love so much that each day,
you're not ready for the sun to set and you can't wait
for the sun to rise.

READY SET CONNECT

I walked into the pastel yellow building on the corner of Adams Avenue in Los Angeles right on the dot for my interview. I had arrived 30 minutes early and waited in my car until 10:59am to execute my perfectly timed 11:00am entrance.

I had just graduated with my bachelor's degree in Communicative Disorders, which put me on track to go to graduate school and become a speech-language pathologist. But I'll be honest: I was not sold on the profession—not by any means. Any time I observed sessions at our on-campus clinic, it just looked like the therapists were playing with the kids. Were they actually getting anything done? Didn't look like it.

Given that I wasn't ready to commit to this profession, graduate school was out. But I had enough hours to apply for my speech-language pathology assistant (SLPA) license and get my toes wet. Test it out and see what all the fuss was about. Plus, I had no other decent options. I decided I would get my assistant license and give that a go.

I moved out to Santa Monica, into a high-rise building that I wouldn't be able to afford for long without a job. I prepared my resume and cover letter and applied to every SLPA or related job I could find on this Earth (within a reasonable distance from Santa

Monica). I blasted out my resume. Crickets. Right as I was going into panic mode, I heard back from a clinic.

So here I am. A bright-eyed, bushy-tailed 22-year-old graduate with ill-fitting business pants and virtually no relevant work experience, on my very first big-girl job interview.

I walked into the clinic and was introduced to the clinic director. While giving me a tour of this massive multidisciplinary clinic, she pointed out what each room was for. "Here's our sensory gym…here's where we run social skills groups…and here are the rooms we use for speech therapy. We do Floortime therapy in those rooms. Do you know what that is?"

"Of course," the words spew out of me uncontrollably without a second passing, followed by immediate regret. "Great!" She seemed pleased. "Because every therapist here also does Floortime sessions."

What is wrong with you? I think. *Mental note: Floortime therapy. You gotta remember that.*

We go back to her office and she sits down at her desk, signaling me to take a seat.

"Here's a printout to show you where we'd start you out in terms of salary, and what benefits we offer. You would be doing a combination of speech therapy, Floortime therapy, and running social skills groups. We'd love to offer you the job."

"I accept!" I squeal. "I am so excited, thank you!" Her eyes widened in surprise. I didn't realize until much later on, when I started interviewing and hiring for my own clinic, that I was maybe the first human on the face of this planet to accept a job 0.5 seconds after it had been offered, with zero follow-up questions.

I walk back to my car with a skip in my step. I take out my brand-new iPhone (this was 2009, people), gently tap the screen, head to Google, and type, "What is Floortime therapy?" And this…is where my story begins.

Part 1:

Ready

How You Can Accelerate Communication
by Focusing on What's Easy

CHAPTER 1

Start Your Engines

Why You Need to Be an Out-of-the-Box Thinker to Best Support Your Kids

Before there was a sensory trained speech-language pathologist (SLP) with a top-ranked therapy clinic, speaking to and training tens of thousands of professionals and families around the globe, there was an insecure speech-language pathology assistant (SLPA) just hoping her supervisor's shadow would drift away from her observation window.

During my time as an SLPA, Floortime, and social skills therapist, I had excellent training and support—more than I appreciated at the time. I had not one, but three incredibly experienced supervisors: one for speech therapy, one for Floortime, and one for social skills. I had weekly meetings with each of my three supervisors, and one additional meeting per week with my mentor, who was a newly licensed SLP. This meant four hours of meetings per week where I was trained in therapy approaches I still rely on heavily today.

One of these approaches was Floortime therapy. I was trained by a mentee of the late Dr. Stanley Greenspan, the creator of Floortime. Floortime is a relationship-based approach that focuses on building engagement, language, and higher-level thinking skills through activities that are intrinsically motivating for kids.

One day of my group training, my instructor pretended to be a busy Autistic child, and our goal was to get her engaged. Normally I'd be quivering at the thought of getting up in front of an audience (I had most certainly outgrown my theater days), but I actually volunteered to go first. I had just learned a ton of early intervention language building strategies and I was excited to show off my skills.

She places two chairs next to each other, as if we're in a toy car. She puts her hands out like they're on the steering wheel, and starts saying "Vroom!" I sit next to her and pull out the language strategy I'd recently learned, giving fill-in the blanks. I excitedly say "Ready...set..." and look at her expectantly. She ignores me, jarring her hands and the pretend steering wheel to the right. I try again, "Ready...set..." I say a little louder this time. She looks at me, picks her chair up from under her, plops it down facing the other direction, and continues with her car noises. I sat there still. I was fresh out of ideas. She sent me back to my seat in the audience. I was mortified. My confidence came to a screeching halt that day.

At some point, we all learn the hard way. We can't become an expert just by reading a textbook. Expertise is not knowledge. It's knowledge *plus* experience. And I was nowhere near the 10,000 hours Malcolm Gladwell argues one would need to call themself an expert (Gladwell, 2008). Three years later, I was presenting nationally alongside Jake Greenspan, son of Dr. Stanley Greenspan, delivering lessons on how to utilize a Floortime-based approach to standing-room-only audiences of therapists. A quick reminder that we all start somewhere

While I was an SLPA, my supervisors carved out time to observe me each month. To most fresh therapists, this would sound like a dream. So many new therapists receive very little supervision and have to go it alone. I don't want to complain, but every time I was supervised, I slowly died inside, bit by bit. I loved the learning—but I dreaded the feeling of incompetence that came along with it. Every time I saw a supervisor's shadow looming over the observation window, I was terrified. It was like my brain stopped functioning (which I understand now as going into fight or flight)—*that's* how horrifying it was for me.

It didn't help that I was the youngest therapist in the clinic. And with my brown curly hair, high-pitched voice, and deep dimples, I still looked like I was in high school. I tried to compensate in other ways. I started straightening my hair to look older. I wore business pants and sweaters even on casual Fridays when everyone else was in jeans and tees.

But the truth is, I wouldn't be where I am today without that year filled with intense supervision and training. And there are kids from whom I learned so much I could never possibly forget them. Like my little friend, Sam.

Sam was a three-year old boy who was non-speaking (back then, we called him nonverbal). I saw him for Floortime therapy. Did I mention our sessions were three hours long?! But the pain was not that I was responsible for this little nugget for a few hours, it was that this meant I had to spend three hours every Monday morning feeling like the most incompetent therapist west of the Mississippi. Three hours of questioning *Why? Why can't I get him to engage with me? Why am I doing this job? Why do I suck at life?*

Every therapist in the clinic knew of little Sam. This adorable golden-haired, blue-eyed boy would jet into the clinic and go in and out of every therapy room. This was the kind of kid whose legs, when he was being carried by his mom, would make those little bicycle kicks mid-air, and then as soon as his tiny feet hit the floor, he was off and he never looked back. This kid gave me a run for my money. Literally.

Week after week, I dreaded going to work, because every Monday from 9am to 12pm I'd be losing my mind trying to figure out how to help this kid. I just couldn't keep him still. Unless he had cars. Then he would lay on his tummy, his head on the ground next to him, driving the cars back and forth, back and forth. And in this case, I had no idea how to get him engaged.

Every month, the clinic's team of about 15 supervisors would get together to watch therapy videos and provide feedback to the therapist. I remember when my Floortime supervisor came up to me and said, "We want to review a video of Sam at next month's meeting." I felt my body physically shutting down. *Him? Of all the kids on my caseload?! It has to be the one kid I have absolutely no idea what I'm doing with?* I begrudgingly agreed. I prayed I could get a reasonable video to submit to them where I appeared to be a half-decent therapist. The pressure was on.

It's Monday, I set up the camera to record. I bring in the CD player (again: 2009, people) and some of his favorite music. He crawls up onto the table where the CD player was and starts changing the songs, pushing button after button. I try dancing behind him. But nope, he doesn't look—the buttons seem to be more exciting than me. I try sticking my face up next to him and making weird noises (seriously, guys, I have this on tape). He keeps changing the song. I start singing, tapping the table, and clapping my hands. He turns and looks at me. I smile and keep bopping along. He stands up on the table, looking down at me smiling. I kneel in front of him and extend my arms. He launches off the table, and crashes into my arms, the momentum making us roll down onto the ground. We're both laughing. He quickly runs back around to climb up on the table, stands up, and reaches toward me. I give him that "expectant wait" look, where I'm looking at him with wide eyes, as if I'm expecting him to take a turn. He says "Go!" This is one of the first words I have ever heard him say. My heart was happy. We do that over and over again. Rinse and repeat. I had never seen him so engaged and connected.

I was beyond excited to get this footage to my supervisor. Everyone at the clinic knew this kid, and they were going to be so impressed. Or so I thought. I submit the tape and eagerly await my judgment. My supervisor starts the feedback session with a question, "Why'd you let him stand on the table?"

"Ummm…" Uh oh here it comes again. This time it was freeze. I was totally thrown off. She went into some spiel about liability and blah blah blah. I honestly don't think I heard any of the words she said. I was too busy shutting down. He was so connected, he was so engaged, he was communicating! Who cares if he was standing on a table? I was so disheartened.

I made a vow to myself that day. I decided that I would always put connection first. I knew that this belief might not be shared by all of the therapists I would encounter along the way, but what I've learned is that sometimes you aren't going to find the key to unlocking a child's communication by staying on the traditional, straight and narrow road. Sometimes that key is two left turns and a tunnel away. And let me ask you, will you ever regret going off the beaten path if it's going to take your kids to where they need to be to learn and grow? I have a feeling that if you are the type of person who is reading this book, you're also the type of person who has seen that traditional approaches either don't work or don't feel good (or both!), and you're ready for something new and different.

Ready Set Connect is designed to provide you with concepts and strategies to strengthen the foundations that need to be in place to build communication. Traditional approaches sometimes feel easier, because most kids will sit at a table and comply if the reward is great enough. However, these teaching methods ultimately make the road longer and harder for you because they disregard the foundational steps that are needed for kids to learn. I'm going to show you how focusing on foundational skills will actually accelerate communication development.

In Part 1: Ready, you'll learn the crucial role that sensory regulation plays in developing engagement and communication, and why our primary focus areas with children should be to build strong, trusting relationships and find activities that are intrinsically motivating.

In Part 2: Set, you'll learn how to support children's regulation, engagement and communication in neurodiversity affirming ways, how to analyze a child's sensory needs, and practical strategies for bringing children into and maintaining a regulated state.

In Part 3: Go, you'll learn three powerful ways to support children's sensory needs and the importance of helping them advocate for their needs. You'll hear from three professionals in different work settings who will give you tips for success with implementing a sensory approach no matter where you are.

At the end of each chapter, you'll find "Your Next Turn", in which I ask you questions to reflect on the chapter. This is designed so that you are able to easily implement what is shared in this book. I highly recommend taking just a few minutes to answer the questions, which will guide you in determining your next action step.

Thank you for being here. The stories I am going to share with you are deeply personal, and bring to light the greatest and hardest moments of my career. I feel honored to share them with you and I hope that this book inspires you to persist on your journey, as you continue to learn how to better support the children in your life.

Never forget that you are making a difference, one child at a time.

Much Love,

Jessie

KEY TAKEAWAYS:

» When you are stuck and feeling like you don't know how to get a child to engage with you, think outside of the box. Take the road less traveled. Don't be afraid to embarrass yourself. You never know what's going to work.

» Always put connection first. Connection opens the door to communication.

Your Next Turn:

Think about when you started your journey. What is one moment that felt incredibly difficult, but helped you to become the therapist or parent you are now?

Who are some of the mentors that led you to where you are today?

Have you downloaded the Free Guidebook that goes along with the book? Go to readysetconnectbook.com to download the Guidebook that will help you implement everything you're learning as you work through this book.

CHAPTER 2

Shifting Gears

The Connection Between Regulation and Communication

A s I continued on my speech therapy journey, I encountered numerous enlightening moments, but none as transformational as my first co-treatment session with an occupational therapist (OT). Those 30 minutes would change the trajectory of my career. It was the lightbulb moment when I realized that sensory strategies should be a part of every speech session.

James was a darling four year old with stick-straight blonde hair that gently covered his brown eyebrows. His mom was a gorgeous ex-model who always enthusiastically participated in his therapy—the type of parent who used me as her own personal therapist. To be honest, I was just honored that she felt like I was credible enough to open up to. After all, I was a sad excuse for an adult with almost no life experience.

For the first five minutes of every one of James' sessions, he would do the same thing: open the door, shut the door, open the door, shut the door, open the door…you get the picture.

He was a pretty quiet kid but super easygoing. He would play with any toy I put in front of him. He didn't initiate much, but he would respond to me fairly consistently. I don't know why, but I just had a feeling that I wasn't seeing him at his best—that I was just scratching the surface of his enormous potential. Session after session, he would just sit and chill with me, sort of playing with whatever toy I presented. He was a textbook "easy" kid, but something was missing.

It all changed the day his OT and I had our first co-treatment session. She put him on the swing, and gave him a huge push. It was like turning on a switch. I could actually see his eyes light up. I had never seen him so engaged and using so much language.

I couldn't understand the phenomenon. Who was this kid in front of me? He was talking more than I'd ever seen in my speech sessions. As I marveled and bubbled up with excitement seeing what James could do, his OT explained sensory regulation to me.

Sensory processing is our ability to register, interpret, and integrate information coming in through our senses. You might hear people say "sensory activities", and I use that phrase too, but in reality every activity is a sensory activity, because our sensory system is constantly working to take in and make sense of stimuli around us. Just as I sit here on a plane now, I hear the gray noise of the airplane. I can feel the leather seat on my shoulder blades. I smell the strange snacks the toddlers across the aisle are eating. I see the brightness from my computer screen. I feel hunger pangs, signaling to me that the $12 cheese plate I just bought didn't quite serve its purpose.

Once you start thinking about sensory input, it's almost like you can't "unsee" it. You start to think about your sensory system every-where you go, because it's such a critical part of day-to-day life.

But why is understanding this so critical to speech therapy? Studies show that up to 95% of Autistic individuals have sensory differences, and this affects how they experience the world (see references). For most neurotypical people, our bodies go through a series of steps when sensory information is presented to us: We detect the input, we adjust and filter the input, we organize it and interpret it, and then we respond. Autistic people often have differences in the way their sensory information is processed, and these differences impact everyday life. For example, they might be processing something in a way that's very different than their neurotypical peers—more or less intense: a sound might feel extra loud, a touch might feel extra uncomfortable. Having one recess break all morning during class might not feel like enough movement for them. The first step in determining what our kids need is to understand their sensory systems, and this starts with understanding our eight senses:

Sight (Visual System)

Ask yourself: What are you looking at right now? Is it dark or light? Do you have a small number of items in your environment or are you in a busy place? Are the objects or people in your environment still or moving?

Hearing (Auditory System)

What sounds do you hear at the moment? People talking? Kids playing? The soft hum of traffic? Your breath? Your fan? Are there competing sounds in the environment?

Touch (Tactile System)

What do you feel right now? Your clothes on your skin? Something under your toes? Your back against a chair? Your fingers on a page? Are these comfortable or comforting feelings, or is something you're touching bothering you slightly?

Smell (Olfactory System)

What smells are in your environment? Food? Furniture? People? Are these smells familiar to you or unfamiliar? Are they evoking any memories? Are they relaxing aromas or are they unpleasant?

Taste (Gustatory System)

What can you taste? Any tastes lingering on your tongue? What tastes are enjoyable to you and which tastes disgust you?

Balance & Movement (Vestibular System)

Are you sitting upright, lounging, or laying down? Is your head tilted to the side? Are you feeling balanced and secure at the moment? Do you feel like you need to get up and move?

Body Awareness (Proprioceptive System)

Are you pushing or pulling on anything at the moment? Pushing your feet against an ottoman? Pushing the pages down with your fingers? Pushing your back into a chair?

Internal Senses (Interoceptive System)

What is your body telling you right now? Does your body need anything? Are you hungry? Are you thirsty? Could you use a trip to the bathroom?

I hope answering the above questions will help you feel more aware of your own sensory systems. Answering these questions can help you feel more in tune with your body and what you need.

But now what? How does understanding the sensory systems help a person to engage, communicate, and learn?

Sensory regulation is our ability to process sensory information, and adjust our levels of arousal, attention, and responses.

What exactly is a person's level of arousal? An individual's arousal level is the state of alertness or wakefulness that they experience, which influences how they respond to the sensory stimuli around them. A person's arousal level can be low (for example, when you feel drowsy), high (for example, when you feel stressed), a mix between these two, or optimal (for example, when you're focused and engaged).

Certain activities might increase our level of arousal (like a roller coaster), while some decrease our level of arousal (like soft music).

Although certain sensory experiences have a similar impact on many people, each individual possesses unique sensory needs. After a long day at work, one person might wind down by taking a long walk outdoors with their dog, while another might plop down on the couch for a couple hours of *Real Housewives*. (Don't ask which one I am.)

Our kids have unique sensory needs too. A session in a small therapy room can be very effective for one child, but make another child feel cooped up and antsy. A session in a big gym could be really exciting and fun for one child, and completely overstimulating and overwhelming for another. Knowing a child's individual sensory needs is one of the keys to designing effective therapy sessions.

James was under-stimulated in our small therapy room. He needed movement and lots of fun visual stimulation, like the gym provided. When he got on the swing, it's almost like he "woke up". His level of arousal increased, his attention increased, and all of a sudden, he was in a regulated and engaged state.

Learning about sensory regulation completely changed the way I was able to work with him, and every other child I worked with after that. I still targeted my language goals, but in a way that gave my clients the input they needed to bring them into their most regulated, ready-to-learn state. This one session opened my eyes to a new perspective of what speech therapy could look like.

One of his goals was to answer WH-questions. Instead of sitting him down at a table, the OT would push him on the swing. I'd hide my childhood beanie babies around the gym while he closed his eyes, and then I'd ask him where they were. (You knew he was special to me if I was willing to put one of my most prized possessions at risk for this learning opportunity…'80s babies, you get it). We flew through those prepositions because he was so regulated, engaged, and motivated.

This innovative approach to speech therapy, which incorporated sensory regulation into the learning process, not only revolutionized my practice, but also significantly enhanced my clients' engagement and communication. I knew that I was going to continue down this road, pedal to the metal.

KEY TAKEAWAYS:

» We have eight sensory systems: Auditory, Tactile, Gustatory, Olfactory, Visual, Vestibular, Proprioceptive, and Interoceptive.

» Sensory regulation is our ability to process sensory information, and adjust our levels of arousal, attention, and responsiveness.

» Our arousal level is our state of wakefulness or alertness.

» Certain activities might increase our arousal level, while some decrease it.

» We all have unique sensory needs. Figuring out a child's unique sensory needs is the first step to building engagement and communication.

Your Next Turn:

Take a moment to think about your own sensory system. What's one sensation you love? Which sensory system is it processed by? What's one sensation that bothers you? Being able to make sense of your own sensory system helps you empathize with those who process sensory information differently.

Inside Out Sensory Trained Therapist Highlight

Before Inside Out, I was at a place in my career where I no longer knew what I wanted to do with speech pathology, and through my own journey of diagnosis, and my son's, I found a whole new passion for sensory and how we can implement this into the speech pathology world. I feel like Inside Out has allowed me to become a better SLP, and with that, I've been able to become a better mother, because being able to understand myself and my sensory needs has allowed me to understand my son's sensory needs better and my clients'. I am able to fully be the neurodiversity affirming therapist I hoped to be, and for that, I am forever grateful to the Inside Out Program.

Bettina Lopez Lam, MS, CCC-SLP, IBCLC, CLC
Autistic SLP & Mom to Autistic Child
Founder of Milk & Hvni Therapy and Consulting / Miss Bee SLP, LLC
@itsannbettina

CHAPTER 3

Filling Up the Tank

Focus on Building Intrinsic Motivation to Facilitate Learning

My sessions didn't look like traditional "speech therapy" anymore. When most people think about speech sessions, they envision a child seated at a table across from a therapist who is holding up flashcards, and structured therapy was very commonly used for Autistic kids at this time. The good news is that, as a field, we are now moving toward more effective approaches that center around the child's interests.

This more traditional, structured type of speech therapy is very often compliance-driven, meaning the goal of the activity is for the child to comply (i.e., complete the activity at hand). This kind of approach typically utilizes reward systems to reach its goal of compliance. For example, telling a child that *first* we are going to look at these pictures and *then* you can have a break. Or *first* you have to get five stars by working and *then* you get to play on the iPad. After the child complies, they are rewarded.

Traditional therapy focuses on extrinsic motivation, whereas this new direction I was heading very much focused on intrinsic motivation. Intrinsic motivation refers to the drive to engage in an activity for the satisfaction that is inherently received from participating in that activity. Extrinsic motivation refers to the drive to engage in an activity for the reward that comes at the end.

The problem with these rewards-based approaches is that, although so much of our world is driven by external rewards (e.g., we work and get a paycheck), research shows that they don't increase intrinsic motivation. Hence, why taking a job just for the paycheck doesn't actually make you happy. There are many other factors that make you more motivated in a job, such as having autonomy over how you do your job, getting lots of learning opportunities to master skills, and having a purpose behind your work (Pink, 2009).

Typically, we use rewards to motivate people, but they actually do the opposite: they decrease intrinsic motivation over time. You might tell your child that after they eat their broccoli, they can have chocolate cake. Will it be effective? Not with my two year old, but probably with my older kids. At least for a while. And while you can likely get your child to eat broccoli with chocolate cake as a reward, it's not going to make them enjoy eating broccoli in the future. You're not raising a broccoli-loving kid for life. In fact, they'll probably go out to eat 20 years later with their friends and say, "Ugh, I hate broccoli. My parents used to force me to eat it growing up."

Alfie Kohn, author of *Punished by Rewards*, once said in an interview, "Rewards are not completely ineffective. They can get one thing under certain conditions—temporary compliance." So while so many therapists utilize reward systems to get their clients to participate in therapy activities, it's not making them more intrinsically motivated to participate in the future.

You might be asking, why does this concern you? Why does it matter if a therapist sits their Autistic client at a table, has them look through picture cards to answer questions, and then rewards them with a sticker?

Well, the answer is simple. This isn't how kids learn best. Kids need to be intrinsically motivated to learn in the most effective way possible. One of my favorite quotes is by Katrina Gutleben who said, "Children need to be motivated in order to learn. If they're not motivated, it's like throwing marshmallows at their head and calling it eating." Without being motivated, it's like we are throwing all of this language at them but they're not actually absorbing, processing, and learning.

Think about it in your own life. You know that age-old argument you have with your spouse? The one that goes something like this:

Honey, did you do the dishes?
No, I didn't know you wanted me to do the dishes.
I don't want to have to ask you. I want you to want to do the dishes.
I'm sorry, why would I want to do the dishes?

At the end of the day, wanting something for someone isn't the way they're going to get it. They have to want it for themselves.

One of my biggest goals in therapy is for my kids to want to be there. I don't want them to participate because they're going to get a sticker or star or five minutes on the iPad. I want them to *want* to participate. Because it's fun. Because they enjoy being around me. Because I make them laugh. Because it *feels good*.

This is why making sure our kids are intrinsically motivated to participate is so critical. So that they can get the most out of their time with us.

By Now You Might Be Thinking, What About the Kids Who Are Unmotivated?

Ugh, one of my biggest pet peeves. No, not the "unmotivated" kids, but the people who call kids "unmotivated". But I won't lie: I've been there, said that.

Kids can't be unmotivated. By definition, all behavior is motivated by something. So it's not that our kids are *unmotivated*, it's just that they're motivated by something other than what we want them to be motivated by (Lavoie, 2007). A child in your session may not be motivated to sit at a table and go through flashcards, but they might be very motivated to lay on the ground and roll cars on the carpet.

What I don't understand is why the onus falls on the child. "The child is unmotivated"—doesn't it make more sense to say our therapy activity isn't motivating for the child? Whose responsibility is it? I like to think it's ours, as the therapist. It's our job to find activities that are highly motivating for kids. And it's our responsibility to know our clients and their goals so well, that it doesn't matter what activity they want to do, because we can target their goals no matter which activity they choose.

One way to make any activity more motivating is by incorporating sensory input. Not only does incorporating sensory input make sessions more fun, but it is also the key to unlocking a child's full communication potential.

My experience with James in the gym that day paved a new road for me, beginning another chapter in my journey as an SLP. Incorporating movement into his therapy activities was not only more motivating because it was fun, but it also gave him the sensory input he needed to be in a more regulated, engaged state.

By this time, after learning about Floortime and sensory regulation, everything had changed for me. My trajectory became clear: I was ready to go to graduate school. I wrote about James and my passion for sensory-based sessions in my Personal Essay for my application. The terrified 22 year old taking a job because it was her only option in fact marked just the beginning of her story.

KEY TAKEAWAYS:

» Historically, compliance-based approaches have been used extensively with Autistic children. While there is currently a shift to more child-led therapy, these structured approaches are still used commonly today.

» Research shows that reward systems decrease intrinsic motivation over time. Children learn best when they are intrinsically motivated.

» Kids can't be unmotivated! Our job is to figure out what motivates them and use this to plan our sessions.

Your Next Turn:

Think about times in the past when you have relied on a reward system with a child. How did you feel while utilizing this type of system to gain compliance? Now think about times where you have thrown the goal of "completing the activity" out the window and just did what was intrinsically motivating for the child. How did that feel?

Inside Out Sensory Trained Therapist Highlight

I struggled with engaging my clients for a sustained amount of time and only really having those short windows of engagement. I also struggled with building a relationship and developing authentic connection before becoming sensory trained. Becoming sensory-informed has completely transformed the way I practice by giving me the tools needed to co-regulate with my clients and help them reach optimal regulation so they could engage authentically during communicative interactions and social experiences. Most importantly, it has impacted the way I see my neurodivergent kids by using a different lens and knowing how to support them so that I can truly support them build their language and total communication. I am so grateful for the opportunity to learn about sensory and how it impacts communication because without that information I would continue to feel stuck.

Louisa Lopez, M.S. CCC-SLP
Founder of Speech and Sensory, LLC
@speechandsensory

CHAPTER 4

Choosing Your Make & Model

It's Time to Find Your Therapy Values

I t was a sunny Monday just after lunch, and I was kneeling down in a mainstream second-grade classroom, frantically picking up the papers and tiny ice cream, cupcake, and assorted other dessert-shaped erasers seven-year-old Autistic Olivia had just thrown all over the floor, right after she flipped her chair back, screaming at the top of her lungs.

This was a prestigious private school, and I was hired as Olivia's 1:1 behavior support therapist. I had no prior training in behavior therapy, but I was in graduate school, in need of a job, and her parents said that her current therapist would train me.

I remember our training sessions. Her therapist had a binder of a bunch of concepts Olivia needed to learn. One concept was the weather. The therapist would ask her, "What's the weather today?" and Olivia wouldn't answer. So she'd ask again, "What's the weather today?" No response. Third time, "What's the weather today?" Then the therapist would prompt her, "The weather is…"—"Raiiiiinnbowwww!" Olivia interjected with a singsong inflection in her voice. "The weather is sunny," her therapist modeled. Then put an "x" next to the weather goal. She said I had to ask Olivia three times, and if she was wrong all three times, to mark it as wrong and try again the next day. She went through her entire binder like that each day.

It actually seemed straightforward, and I kind of liked that. Try three times, she gets it wrong all three times, move on. It was easy for me. But it was not fun for Olivia. I wondered how she was actually going to learn these concepts, as they had been working on them for years already.

I was hired to be with her during her school day. I'd spend the morning with her and her 1:1 special education teacher who was privately hired, then I'd spend the afternoons with her in her second-grade class. Which was about the least fun place to be.

Essentially, my job was to keep her disruptive behaviors to a minimum in the classroom so that she didn't distract her peers.

While that seemed like a manageable task, every few minutes she would do something that inevitably turned heads: throwing her papers on the ground, yelling out loud, or tipping her chair back so far that she would flip over. It was clear that she did not want to be in that classroom. And to be honest, neither did I.

I can't even count the number of times a day I would say "Quiet hands" or "Quiet mouth," as I was instructed to do.

If you're not familiar with these prompts, they are very commonly used in compliance-based therapy. Oftentimes, Autistic children engage in self-stimulatory behaviors, called stimming. Stimming usually involves repetitive body movements. The prompt "quiet hands" is often used to get kids to stop stimming and sit still so they can pay attention. And while I knew a little about sensory regulation at this point, I wasn't too stim savvy. I didn't know much about the purpose stimming serves. It's often a sign that a child is trying to self-regulate, and it's therefore not something we should discourage or try to eliminate.

So there I would sit, in the back row of the class with her, her reward chart in front of her on her desk, as I would say "Quiet hands," "Quiet body," or any other prompts I needed to try to get her to stay still and participate in the classroom activities. It didn't feel good.

Then recess would come around. And I would go rogue. Her parents and therapists didn't give me any explicit instructions for recess, which meant I would just focus on sensory regulation and engagement. While her other therapists would only let her swing for a count of 100, I would let her swing for 20 minutes. I can still see her in her red sweater (a signature piece of her school uniform), her blonde hair in a ponytail with a red and blue plaid ribbon, the sun glimmering in her blue eyes, and her smile so wide while the wind moved across her face as she flew back and forth on the swing and I recited all of her favorite rhymes with her.

Then we would go into an empty classroom and all I would focus on was engagement. I just wanted to connect with her, plain and simple. And that's where she would shine.

She used to sit on my lap on a spinning chair and we'd take turns singing every other line of "You've Got a Friend in Me". I had taught her the words. She would have the biggest smile as she nestled her little button nose on my cheek. She seemed so happy in those moments it made me want to cry.

Every day I felt so torn. Here I was using these behavioral management strategies that her whole team felt was best for her. Placing the reward chart in front of her so that she always knew what she was "working for". Using verbal prompts to try to get her to keep her body still. All the while, she would yelp out—it's the best way I can describe it. She wasn't actually learning anything. I was miserable. But the worst part was that *she* was miserable.

After these massively structured, compliance-based activities, she'd have unstructured playtime and recess, where I'd completely switch gears to a child-led, connection-driven approach. And we'd have these moments of pure joy and connection that were so beautiful.

It was in that job that I learned the hard but very necessary lesson that, if it doesn't feel good to you, then it probably doesn't feel good to the child either. And it's more than likely not the approach you should be taking.

It's really hard for us when we're in a position where our values are misaligned with the values of our work setting. We can only be happy for so long. Eventually we have to move on to find something that's a better fit for us—for our own emotional health and happiness. But what about the kids who we leave behind? We will never forget them.

It was such a learning experience for me. Sometimes you don't know what isn't a good fit until you try it out. I knew from then on that I would only be happy in a job where I got to use that play-based approach that I so strongly believed in.

A play-based approach is first of all child-led. This means that the child takes an active role in the direction of the play, and the therapist prioritizes the child's interests during sessions. Second, the approach centers around play. The therapist believes that play is the best form of learning, and that learning should happen through play. In play-based approaches, the goal is not compliance, the goal is connection. Play-based therapists know that children learn when they are engaged and interacting. Therefore, building a strong relationship is a crucial piece of the therapeutic process.

I never took a job that didn't align with my values ever again.

KEY TAKEAWAYS:

» We feel more fulfillment when we're in a work setting that is aligned with our values.

» A play-based approach is child-led, prioritizes learning through play, and focuses on building strong connections.

Your Next Turn:

Consider if there has been a time when you felt like your work setting did not align with your values. How did you feel in that situation? Do you think that your values are aligned with your work setting now?

Want help figuring out your own therapy core values?

Go to: www.readysetconnectbook.com to download the Ready Set Connect Guidebook where you can find an exercise to help you think about your own core values.

Inside Out Sensory Trained Therapist Highlight

Understanding how to support children with sensory needs and differences has transformed my speech therapy approach. Early in my career, I felt discouraged when I lacked the tools to effectively support children who were often dys-regulated or "seemed" regulated but plateaued in their progress. Now, after learning about a sensory-informed approach from Jessie, I'm empowered to see the whole child, address their foundational regulatory needs, and more effectively support their higher-level speech and language goals!

Emily Byers Chaney
Speech & Language Program Director at Pediatric Therapy Playhouse
@ndaffirming.slp

CHAPTER 5

Revving the Engine

Trust as the Foundation

After graduate school, I had secured a clinical fellowship (my first real SLP job) in San Diego, when my then-boyfriend got accepted into Georgetown Law School. It was too good of an opportunity to pass up, so we decided we would move out to Washington DC basically overnight.

I was so excited that I busted out my computer, made a list of every private practice in DC, and sent them my resume. There was just one problem: I had forgotten to change the practice name for each email. So 20 emails said that I would love to work at Capitol Hill Pediatrics…but 19 of those clinics were not Capitol Hill Pediatrics.

Needless to say, these DC clinics were "not hiring". Fortunately, Virginia and Maryland were just a short drive away, so I expanded my clinic search. I took a much more cautious approach to emailing this time around.

I discovered that the Floortime Center was in Maryland, only 20 minutes from our apartment. After several rounds of interviews, they offered me a job.

It was a dream job. Not only was it the one and only Floortime Center, run by the son of arguably one of the most influential Autism researchers that ever lived, but I'd be working alongside these internationally renowned professionals, and there were so many hands-on training opportunities.

And what did I do? I turned it down.

I didn't want to work with Autistic kids.

Ok, I said it.

I was terrified. I thought it would be too hard. I didn't feel prepared to work with Autistic kids. I didn't think I was good enough. I didn't think I could give them the kind of therapy they deserved.

I took a job at another private practice. My supervisor saw how much I knew about working with Autistic clients. After all, I had a good amount of training and experience by then. But I struggled to see it in myself until she pointed it out to me. She asked me to train the whole team.

I started seeing a lot of Autistic kids at this practice and really refined my connection-driven approach. I learned that developing a meaningful relationship with a client is far more important than anything else we could possibly do. And one of the kids who taught me that lesson was sweet, green-eyed, dirty-blonde Josh.

Four-year-old Autistic Josh was sitting on my lap and I could have cried. His mom was dying, and he didn't know it.

When I met Josh I knew his mom had a degenerative disease. But I didn't know she would pass away within the year. I knew he must have been going through a lot emotionally, even though he didn't verbalize it.

So what did I do? I loved that kid so hard I basically treated him like he was mine.

He'd come in for sessions. First thing, he would sit on my lap facing me and we'd talk. We'd talk about our days. I'd tell him what I did that day. And I'd ask him what he did that day. When we started this routine, he couldn't tell me—he didn't have the language. But I would talk to him like any other kid. That's how we always started our sessions.

I remember the first day he answered a 'what' question. Something clicked for him that day, and his language skyrocketed over the next several months.

I'll never forget the day we were on the dark blue mats in the gym and we were playing with beanie babies, pretending to go to the store. We had just finished pretend shopping at the grocery store and our beanie babies were on their way back to their house. He said they were going to go to bed when they got home. I took my brown teddy bear beanie baby to face his and whined, "I'm too hungry to sleep!" I paused. He took more time to process and respond than most of my other kids. And just when most therapists would probably throw in a prompt for him, I waited some more. And after about 10 seconds he took his white teddy bear beanie baby and said in the sweetest voice, "But I'm too sleepy to eat."

I could not believe I had just gotten that interaction on camera. I probably would have thought it was all in my head if not. I've watched it more times than I can count over the years. My mind was just absolutely blown. This was a kid who, just months before, wasn't answering "what" questions, and by now he had this beautiful abstract language. Just wow.

Fast forward to the day he was sitting on my lap and I was on the verge of tears. I knew his mom's health was declining and he was displaying lots of challenging behaviors at school.

That day he told me about how he didn't want to go into the classroom because there was a fan in there and it was too loud—so he cried and kicked the wall.

I couldn't believe he could now verbalize his sensory needs to me. And more than anything, I couldn't believe that this child I met just six months before was the same kid as the one in front of me that day.

Trust is the foundation of everything with your kids. When kids feel safe, they are more likely to share their thoughts, take risks, and ask questions without having fear of judgment or negative consequences.

Trust is the foundation of everything with your kids.

Increasing trust strengthens relationships. Strong connections and reciprocal interactions promote language development. After a child builds language, we can take that language to build self-advocacy skills. And being able to stand up for what they need and want are skills that will completely change a child's life. Just like for Josh, who sat in the gym that day telling me about why he was upset at school.

And the vow to myself that day: I will love my kids like my own, and I will make sure that they always feel safe with me.

I knew that these philosophies of putting connection first, supporting regulation, staying aligned with my values, and building trust would always be at the forefront of my work moving forward. And one day, as I was sitting on the floor of my therapy room with my laptop on the kid-sized table next to me, right after we found out that my then-fiancé and I needed to move back to Los Angeles for his job, I decided I would go for it. It was time to take everything I'd learned and start a practice of my own.

I battled feeling slightly delusional, considering I had just finished my clinical fellowship. But something in my heart told me that I could do it. All I needed was a little validation, and somehow I would find it. Eventually.

And although I figured now was as good of a time as ever to take the leap, many disagreed with me, including a professor who told me it was disrespectful to our profession to open a private practice so quickly.

I was getting a lot of "no's" and "don'ts"—but all it took was that one "yes" to convince me to make it happen.

"You've got the fire, girl. Go for it." It was the familiar voice of my former professor on the line. This was not the type of professor who shows up, teaches class, and sends students on their merry way. Angela was the type of professor who knew every detail about your life, what the last argument with your best friend was about, and she was most certainly going to barre class with you after lectures. I spent a year under her supervision at her clinic, and she knew me well. That was the one 'yes', the only 'yes' I needed to feel confident in my decision.

Naming my practice was easy. I wanted the name of my practice to reflect my love of child-led therapy, but also wanted it to sound like an inviting place for kids. So I settled on Pediatric Therapy Playhouse, so that families could tell their kids, "We're going to the Playhouse!" My friend whipped up an adorable logo, and what followed was a lot of slightly less easy steps, like renting a commercial property, and then renovating that property (with my dad's help). I forged ahead, step by step.

As I built my practice, I learned the hard way that it was too difficult to be good at everything. Eventually I honed my skills and continued to focus on working with young Autistic children.

One day, I was sitting at my desk in my less-than-impressive, darker-than-it-should-be, rundown office, when I got an email from a publisher. The email read, "Because of your expertise in social communication, we would love for you to contribute to our textbook." Me? An expert? It was a look-over-your-shoulder-moment. A kind of moment when you think the cute guy in the coffee shop is waving to you, and you check that it's not just because his drop-dead girlfriend is actually standing right behind you. That email request really threw me off, because I didn't see myself as an expert. It's one of those moments that led me to realize, *I guess I do kind of have a lot of experience in this area.* The next few years were one big blur. It all happened so fast. I started hiring therapists, writing for the national magazine, and presenting at the state and national levels. I had one big motivator: I wanted all SLPs to understand the importance of a play-based approach for Autistic children. One training at a time. One article at a time. Onward and upward.

KEY TAKEAWAYS:

» Trust is the foundation for building language.
» Building a strong connection with your clients is one of the most powerful focuses you can have as a therapist.

Your Next Turn:

Think about the role that trust plays in building relationships. Has there been a time where a personal relationship was stifled because you did not have a solid foundation of trust, or perhaps trust was broken? When it comes to therapy, do you feel that you put trust at the forefront of your therapy?

Want some tips on simple ways to build trust with children?

Go to: www.readysetconnectbook.com to download the Read Set Connect Guidebook where you can find some easy trust-building tips.

Inside Out Sensory Trained Therapist Highlight

Like many SLPs and SLPAs, I've faced challenges in my career. An area I consistently struggled with was managing behaviors, like meltdowns, distractibility, and eloping, to name a few. But despite my best efforts, I found it challenging to understand and address these issues until I was introduced to sensory approaches. During the height of the pandemic, I decided to take a deep dive into sensory approaches. I stumbled upon Jessie's free videos of how to use sensory strategies as an SLP. Those videos inspired me and I implemented the little nuggets I learned from Jessie into my work. And just from the free videos she shared, the results were instant. I was amazed at the positive impact that sensory approaches could have on speech and language therapy. I invested in the Sensory Course for SLPs which proved to be a game changer for me. The course has brought so much fruit into my sessions, and gave me a newfound confidence in my methodologies. I gained a new perspective and a new set of tools to help me manage behavior more effectively and I am now connecting with my clients on a deeper level.

Maribeth Molina, BS, SLPA
Clinic-Based SLPA

CHAPTER 6

Making a U-Turn

A Connection-Centered Approach

It's been five years since I opened my practice, and I'm sitting in my new corner office on a Friday afternoon. The sunlight is shining in, and a client's mother is sitting in front of me with tears in her eyes. She cried, "I'm asking for your advice as a mother. Mother to mother, what should I do?" Her two-year-old son had recently been diagnosed with autism and she desperately wanted to help him.

I met Ahmed when he was two. He came into my therapy room, alongside his mother, her assistant, and a prominent developmental psychologist in Los Angeles. This was a high-powered family: they were living in the United States, but the little boy's father was a government official from another country.

As I was talking to his mom and the psychologist who had recently assessed him, he laid on the floor watching a water bottle roll back and forth. There was no shortage of toys available—I could stock a few Walmarts with all of the toys in my clinic. But there he laid, on the floor, toys all around him, focused on this water bottle. Back and forth, back and forth. For almost an hour.

After meeting the family, I go to observe the little boy in an early intervention program at a well-known center. As I peek through the observation window, I'm horrified by what I see.

Ahmed has a 1:1 aide, as do all of the other two-year-old children in the center. His aide stands behind him, like a puppeteer, controlling every movement of this little guy.

The aide sits him down at a little table and straps him into the matching wooden chair with a leather seatbelt. She drags a puzzle from the other side of the table and parks it in front of him, taking the pieces out. She instructs him to put the pieces into the puzzle. He picks one up and starts banging it on the table. Seated behind him, she quickly places her hand on top of his, and moves his hand until the puzzle piece drops into place. She manually guides his hand to grab another puzzle piece. It slips out of his hand and falls to the floor. She immediately grabs his hand, pulls his body down sideways, and helps him pick up the puzzle piece to bring back to the table. All this time, he has been whining and squirming.

I was really upset when I left the observation. Did this aide not realize that kids don't learn through hand over hand prompting? And on top of that, it was such a violation of his bodily autonomy. She controlled him the whole time like a puppet. He didn't have any governance over his own body.

He starts seeing me for speech sessions, and we have a rough start. When you start working with a child who is so used to these compliance-based approaches, it often inhibits progress. It's like two people sitting in a boat with their backs to each other rowing in different directions. The philosophies are just so different that the child has trouble knowing what's expected of them. When a child is used to compliance-based sessions, they learn that when they are with a therapist it is to "work". They automatically assume this is not going to be fun, and that interferes with the therapeutic relationship that is so important for successful sessions.

The day that his mother came to me in tears, asking, "Mother to mother, what should I do?" hit me hard for some reason. Since becoming a mom, I'd never had a family ask me for advice *as a parent*. I was always getting asked for my advice as a therapist, but never as a mother.

All of a sudden, I realized something: I wasn't giving this family the same advice I would give myself. What would I do if it was my son who had just received an autism diagnosis? What would *I* do? I was doing a disservice to that family by not fully expressing my opinion about how his other therapies were negatively impacting him. He didn't need compliance-based therapy, he needed relationship-based therapy.

He stops attending sessions at the compliance-based center where I'd observed him and begins to attend a local preschool. I start to work with the other therapists who are seeing him, and we hold big meetings with his occupational therapist, music therapist, preschool teacher, psychologist, and his parents.

I increase the intensity of our services and start seeing him three times a week. I stop focusing on building language. I focus on building a connection and a strong relationship. We slowly work hard to strengthen his trust and to undo the trauma he'd experienced in the center. We sing, we dance, we do a ton of sensory-based activities.

One day when we are in a session, I kneel in front of my desk where my computer is so that I can add something to his progress note. I pause from typing and look back over my shoulder to check on him. There he is, across the room, just smiling at me, his big, bright, deep brown eyes shining with joy. He is eagerly waiting for me to finish typing so that we can keep playing.

We started to share moments like that all the time. Even if we were on different sides of the room, he'd look over just to shoot me a smile. He'd run up to me just to hug or cuddle.

And guess what? He was learning new words all the time. I didn't have to work to build his language. With this kind of approach, the learning was coming naturally.

KEY TAKEAWAYS:

» Connection-centered approaches are an effective and meaningful way to build language.
» Families are an integral part of the therapeutic process, and collaboration with families makes a significant difference in a child's progress.
» A child makes more progress when their therapists and team are all on the same page and utilizing the same approach.

Your Next Turn:

Consider the types of approaches you have used in therapy. Have you noticed more progress in your clients when you have moved from a compliance-based approach to a connection-centered approach?

Want some quick ways to strengthen connections in kids?

You can find some easy-to-use strategies in your Ready Set Connect Guidebook.

Don't have the Guidebook yet?

Go to: www.readysetconnectbook.com and you can download it for free.

Inside Out Sensory Trained Therapist Highlight

After 40+ years as an SLP in virtually every setting imaginable, I've seen the whole trajectory of approaches. I love how Inside Out comes back around to this more naturalistic play & engagement...but with a deep focus on sensory needs.

When I started the sensory course, I was thinking 'Well, I'm really pretty good at getting my clients engaged, but there's a piece I'm missing,' which was that regulation piece.

I really feel like this course has taken me to that bottom step where it starts with regulation. Even after 40+ years, that bottom step has never been so solid for me as it is now.

Melanie Peacock Shell, M.Ed, MS, CCC-SLP
SLP of 40+ Years & Inside Out Parent Program Advisor

PART 2:

Set

—————

The Life-Changing Strategies You Never Knew You Needed and Now You'll Never Be Able to Live Without

CHAPTER 7

Starting on the Right Track

Climbing the Language Staircase

A tall man in his mid-forties is standing with his back against my office wall, arms crossed, scratching his scraggly brown hair, and I can't help but notice he is unintentionally making his glasses slowly move up and down. As I'm chasing his two-year-old son Ryder around the room, doing everything in my power to engage him during our first session while simultaneously verbalizing what I'm observing, he's staring through the windows as the orange-pink sunset drifts away. And then he mutters something I'll hear again hundreds of times—maybe even thousands—over the course of my career working with Autistic children (or soon-to-be-diagnosed Autistic children like Ryder): "I don't understand: he knows so many words, why doesn't he use them?"

He looks bewildered as he pushes his shoulders back against the wall and slowly lowers himself until he's seated on the floor, his arms resting on his bent knees. "He knows I'm his dad, but why does he only say 'Dad' sometimes? He knows a dog says 'woof', so why has he only said it once? He knows those are cars," he says, pointing to the usual traffic jam down on Santa Monica Boulevard, "but he's never said the word 'car'."

I take a deep breath and say "Ok..." as I let out a big exhalation. I hop up and grab a piece of paper and a pen from my desk, and sketch a schematic staircase going from the bottom left of the paper up to the top right.

"Picture language development as a staircase. The bottom step is regulation," I say as I write the word below the step. "Think of that as Ryder's ability to be calm and his ability to pay attention. Next, we have a child's ability to engage with others." I write 'engagement' under the second step.

"Now the middle of the staircase I like to call 'basic language'—a child's ability to say words or talk about what they see. And the top steps represent a child's higher-level language and cognitive skills, like abstract thinking."

I draw a strong line going diagonally from the bottom left to the top right. "The banister represents intrinsic motivation. We know that kids will participate in activities if they are rewarded, which is a form of extrinsic motivation. But in order for kids to truly learn, we want them to be intrinsically motivated. In other words, a child can climb to the top of the staircase without holding on to the banister, but we know the safest, fastest, and most secure way to climb to the top is by holding on to the banister— that is, when the child is intrinsically motivated." The dad starts to look slightly overwhelmed, so I tell him, "We'll talk more about that later.

LANGUAGE
STAIRCASE

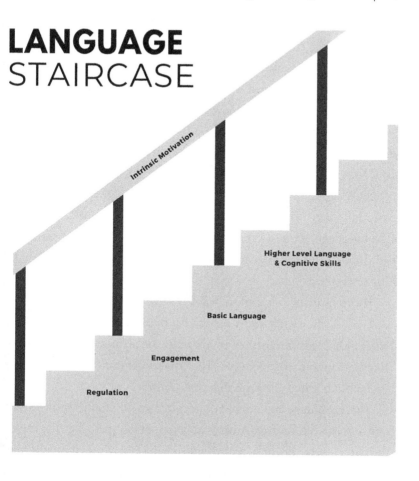

"So often kids come in for speech therapy, like Ryder, and they're not talking, so what would many therapists do? They would say, 'Well, this kid's not talking and it's my job to get them to talk so we better start working on language.' They jump straight to the middle of the staircase," I say, pointing to the 'basic language' step on my drawing.

"There's just one problem: they've forgotten to address these foundational skills that are critical for developing language. And those foundational skills are regulation, engagement, and motivation."

I explain to the dad that we can take virtually any child and use compliance-based approaches to get them to say words. I can put a child in a chair and drill them to say "juice" or "I want to juice." But is that what we want? My goal is not to get kids to say, "I want train." My goal is to get kids to say, "I heard that new Spiderman movie is really good, do you think we can go after school?"

Do you see the difference?

Starting at the middle of the staircase is a great way to elicit basic language. But if we want to truly build flexible, self-initiated language, we need to stabilize the foundation of the staircase. Building a solid foundation is the only way we are going to get our kids to the top.

If the bottom steps aren't stable, we've got to start there.

I ask Dad which steps he thinks need to be more stable for Ryder. Dad confidently points to the bottom steps as he says, "Regulation and engagement. That makes so much sense. No one has ever explained it to me like that before."

The Language Staircase became my go-to analogy for parent training for all of my Autistic clients or soon-to-be-diagnosed Autistic clients. From a neurological point of view, it made perfect sense that we need to be regulated, engaged, and motivated in order to learn. But it also gave me a justification for why my therapy looked the way it did.

Whereas traditional, compliance-based therapy focused so much on language and trying to get kids to say words, my therapy focused on building regulation and engaging my clients in meaningful interactions. It didn't look like traditional therapy, and it's not uncommon for therapists to tell me, "I feel bad not working on language…the parent is going to be wondering what I'm doing." But this simple, clear, and very relevant analogy is all it takes for parents to go from the confused "I don't understand how this play is going to help my child talk" to "These are the foundational skills my child needs in order to talk."

After years of using this analogy, I decided to write about it for the *American Speech Language Hearing Association Magazine*. It was on a whim that I submitted the idea. With every new therapist I trained in my clinic saying "Ahhh," and with every parent who said, "It just makes so much sense," it felt like more professionals would benefit from knowing it, and that they could use it with families too.

When the article was accepted I was 25% excited and 75% terrified. This felt very different from all of the other scholarly articles that our national publication usually puts out there. I was mostly nervous because I was putting my heart on the line. I so deeply believed what I was writing: that focusing on regulation and connection is the most important part of our job, because it leads to more communication. I wasn't a researcher, and I didn't have thousands of perfectly executed trials to back up my ideas. I only had my own experience, and the trends I'd seen consistently over my years of practice. In this article, I felt like I was bearing it all. I was letting the nation into my world.

I'll never forget the day it was published. When you write for this magazine, as the author you always provide your email address at the end of the article. Now, I'd written articles for this magazine in the past, and guess how many emails I'd received? That's right, zero. But not this time.

The day it came out, my inbox was flooded with messages from therapists all over the U.S. They wanted me to know that they felt it was so important to focus on building a connection too—and they thought they were the only ones. They said they always knew in their heart that kids needed to be regulated to get the most out of sessions, but they never knew those terms and had never been able to put it into words. They said their workplaces didn't condone this type of child-led therapy, but it is the type of therapy that feels right to them. They wanted more resources. They wanted to know *how* to address these foundational skills.

But why did this article, out of all articles, pique the interest of so many therapists?

Often times, when SLPs attend seminars, the speaker talks about theory for the entire presentation and saves practical application for the last ten minutes. I see this changing now, but at this time, it was not uncommon for therapists to walk away from seminars saying, "Ok, now what? How do I implement what I just learned on Monday morning?"

In this article I taught application. I concisely explained the why behind the approach (the theory) and then quickly shifted into practice, providing specific examples of how therapists could implement these strategies, starting immediately. And this is something that therapists needed. It was something that they could walk into therapy and start using the next day. No hoops to jump through. Just strategies that would absolutely transform their therapy sessions.

But the most important result of this article was that it let therapists know that there were other professionals on this Earth who believed what they believed, and since it was coming from our national magazine, it felt like they were finally allowed to feel that way. It was ok for therapy to be play-based, relationships-centered, and focused on regulation. And now that they knew there were others, they wanted to know how they could start implementing this type of approach. But this was a lot of new information, and they didn't have any guidance. They didn't know how to begin. So I decided it was time for me to get in the driver's seat and deliver this knowledge. Sensory regulation is the bottom step of the staircase, a key foundation of building a child's communication, and SLPs needed to understand this. These ideas didn't come out of thin air. It's neurology.

When I teach the Language Staircase to parents, therapists, and other professionals, I don't feel like it has to be justified... because it's neurology. This is how our brains work. And there's plenty of science, research, and data to back that up.

One of the simplest explanations I've read comes from Daniel J. Siegel and Tina Payne Bryson's groundbreaking book, *Whole Brain Child*. They describe the brain as having a downstairs (which includes the brainstem, limbic system, and amygdala) and upstairs (cerebral cortex). While the downstairs brain is responsible for automatic, reflexive responses like breathing, instincts like fight or flight, and strong emotions such as fear and anger, the upstairs brain is responsible for higher-level cognitive skills such as planning, problem solving, and decision making. Essentially the upstairs brain allows us to think before we act, and the downstairs brain allows us to act before we think.

UPSTAIRS
BRAIN

Functions:
- Executive functions
- Logic, problem solving, & decision making
- Empathy & morality
- Creativity
- Self-awareness

DOWNSTAIRS
BRAIN

Functions:
- Survival instincts like breathing, heart rate & sleeping
- Fight, flight, freeze, & fawn threat responses
- Emotions
- Automatic responses & behaviors
- Regulation of bodily functions

Now, when we're dysregulated or stressed, it's as if there's a baby gate that shuts between the downstairs brain and upstairs brain. We're trapped in the downstairs brain (Siegel & Bryson, 2011). We can't access our higher-level cognitive skills.

So it is no wonder that when kids are constantly dysregulated, they are having a difficult time attending and learning. They're stuck in their downstairs brain. Language, thinking, and learning aren't functions of the downstairs brain—they are functions that require immense cognitive skills. We need kids to be regulated so that the baby gate barricade opens and they can access the functions their brains have upstairs.

Embarrassing as it is to say, when I started using the Language Staircase analogy when working with parents, I didn't even know that there was an abundance of research that supported it. All I knew was that over my ten-year history of working with Autistic kids, I saw this pattern: that when kids are regulated, engaged, and motivated, we make more progress in therapy, and this approach feels good to families, kids, and me.

It wasn't until my journey to create resources for our therapists that I landed on piles of research supporting this idea: that we have to be regulated in order to use and learn language. And this completed my triangle of Evidence-Based Practice, the greatest support for any therapy approach. If you're not familiar with that, let me explain.

It is drilled into our heads, in graduate school and beyond, that good therapists always use evidence-based practices (EBP). EBP is made up of three components: evidence (aka research, data), clinical expertise (the therapist's experience), and client perspectives (the beliefs and values of the client and their family).

EVIDENCE-BASED
PRACTICE

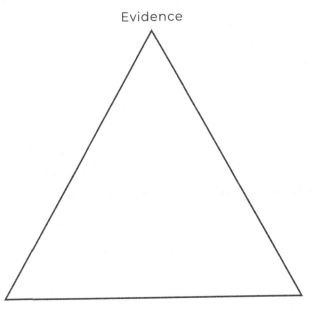

Evidence

Clinical
Expertise

Client Values &
Perspectives

Based on my clinical expertise, I could see that this approach worked.

Based on my clients' perspectives, this approach worked and it felt good to them.

Based on evidence, this approach works: it's neurology.

EVIDENCE-BASED
PRACTICE

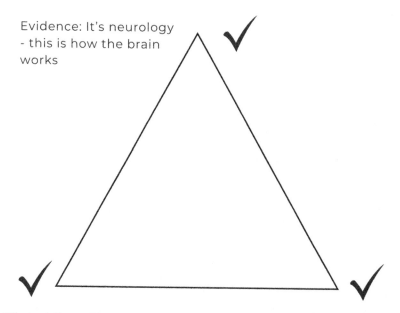

Evidence: It's neurology
- this is how the brain
works

Clinical Expertise:
Based on my
experience, this
works

Patient Values:
This approach
feels good to
families

I was on a mission to start building an online community of like-minded therapists who were passionate about starting at the bottom of the staircase. Therapists who were ready to put regulation first. Therapists who cared more about connecting with their clients than ticking a box on a progress note at the end of the day that said they completed an activity from start to finish. Therapists who knew that prioritizing regulation and connection was ultimately what was going to create the most progress in their clients.

So that's what I did. I hopped online. I started sharing my stories. And slowly I started to find my people. As my practice grew, my online presence grew as well. I spent equal amounts of time working with clients in my clinic, developing resources to use in my clinic, and then—once they were trialed and tested—sharing them with other therapists online.

It was happening. I slowly started to see other drivers going the same direction as me.

KEY TAKEAWAYS:

» Language development is like a staircase, and the bottom step is regulation.

» Once we can stabilize the bottom step of regulation, we can more effectively help the child move up the staircase.

» When our kids are dysregulated, their brain goes into survival mode, and they don't have the ability to use higher-level language and critical thinking skills.

» When our kids are regulated, they're able to access the higher-level thinking parts of their brain.

Your Next Turn:

Think about how the Language Staircase may affect the way you conduct your therapy, or the main points of focus of your therapy. When you were reading about the Language Staircase, did a specific child come to mind? Can you think of a child you used to see, or see currently, who needs therapy focused on the bottom steps of the staircase?

P.S. Want my Language Staircase Assessment, which helps you determine which steps you need to be focusing on with a child?

Go to: www.readysetconnectbook.com to grab your Guidebook, where you'll find my Language Staircase Assessment plus lots of other tools to help you implement what you're learning in this book.

Inside Out Sensory Trained Therapist Highlight

Prior to becoming sensory trained, I did not fully appreciate the deep connection between sensory processing and communication and it was not at the forefront of my mind like it should have been. Once you go through the training, you cannot really think about anything but that connection. Now I start each evaluation and therapy session by making sure my clients' sensory preferences are being met so that they are in their optimal learning zone when I am working on communication goals. Every single one of my clients has benefitted from my sensory training, whether we are working on expressive language or speech sound production.

Alison Moulton, MS, CCC-SLP
Founder and Owner Alison Moulton Speech, Language, and Learning PLLC
@moultonspeech

CHAPTER 8

Dodging Potholes

Are You With Them or Against Them?

When the pandemic hit, SLPs all over the world went into fight or flight. All of a sudden, therapists who struggled to engage their clients even with hands-on therapy activities in a clinic had to start seeing all of their kids virtually. If they didn't feel their in-person therapy was as effective as they wanted it to be, how could they possibly be effective in their therapy approaches through a screen?

I sat in the beige armchair in the dingy apartment I had recently moved into post-divorce. I had just put my two boys to bed and was scrolling through social media. My feed was littered with frantic therapists who were all asking the same question: *What in the world are we going to do?*

To this day I can't tell you why this idea came over me. I heard recently that most of the big decisions that shape your life are the ones you put little to no thought into, and here's a prime example of that: this decision I made within a split second to post in a big group forum. It's not like I had bandwidth for anything else in my life. I had recently been divorced. It was a pandemic. I was taking care of two young kids with spotty childcare. I was dealing with convincing a team of therapists in my clinic that they were going to be fully capable tele-therapists.

But as I sat there, reading these posts of SLPs who were throwing their hands up in the air and seriously considering quitting and collecting unemployment instead, I guess I just couldn't help myself. I posted in a big group asking: "If I go live tomorrow and talk about how to do teletherapy with Autistic kids who need a high level of support, would you come?" (I actually didn't post that. I said "Low functioning kids with autism"—but changed it to more neurodiversity affirming language here. More on this soon.)

Why I chose TOMORROW out of all days is a mystery to me. It was already 9pm. Did I not want to give myself more than 12 hours to prepare something, considering I had not one idea about what I was going to say when I posted that? I don't know what I was thinking. But the reaction was overwhelming. Responses poured in. So many therapists said they would attend.

The next day, I was in my office with a whiteboard on a live training with hundreds of SLPs who were extremely grateful to be learning how to support their Autistic clients virtually.

I taught them about my approach of putting regulation first. I taught them strategies to engage their clients, and how to coach parents. It was revolutionary for them (their words). Most SLPs at this point had very little knowledge of sensory strategies and how important it is to support a child's regulation in order to get them engaged and communicating. I gave them numerous handouts I'd created in the past that I used in my own clinic. And they were hungry for more.

I started putting out tons of free content to support therapists working with Autistic children. Videos, blogs, and assessments.

Some sessions were still virtual, while some of us were shifting back to in-person sessions in our inordinately sanitized clinics. Most therapists were being taught that they should sit their Autistic clients at a table and show them enlarged pictures of kids' dramatic faces and have them guess what they were feeling and why, with a token board by their side. I was teaching them to do the opposite. Sit on the floor. Pick their kids up. Jump around with their kids. Be a kid too.

While the world was focused on compliance, structure, and rote memorization, I was focused on regulation, engagement, and intrinsic motivation. Therapists loved this change of pace. Just like when I started switching directions earlier in my career, this felt really good to them. They felt like they were making a difference while also respecting their kids' needs. They felt like they were supporting their kids to grow and learn while also building strong connections and meaningful relationships. They were happier at work. Their kids were happier in therapy.

During a lunch break in the midst of a busy day of clients, I am catching up on posts in my online group. As I am scrolling through new comments on a video I had posted, my stomach drops while reading one of the responses. It was an Autistic SLP telling me that if I respected my clients I would use identity-first language (using the term "Autistic child") instead of person-first language (using the term "child with autism"). To say I am defensive is an understatement. I vehemently reject her recommendation. After a few more conversational exchanges, she provides me with some resources, and this is when I truly understand the impact behind my language.

Person-first language was all the rage starting in the '70s. It was part of the self-advocacy disability movement, and using person-first language was meant to indicate *This is a person first, their disability comes second.* This was heavily championed by various disabled communities.

In the '90s, the neurodiversity movement emerged, which sought to embrace individual differences. The neurodiversity paradigm takes it be axiomatic that there is no one right way of thinking or being. In other words, there are not "good brains" or "bad brains". Neurodivergent brains are not deficient or defective, they simply function differently.

Identity-first language began to be embraced by the Autistic community (using the term "Autistic person"). Identity-first language says *Autism is a valuable piece of this person that should be embraced. We cannot separate Autism from the person.*

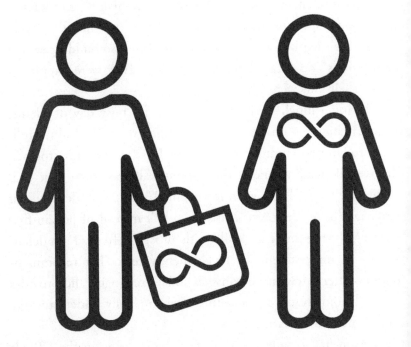

"I HAVE AUTISM"   "I AM AUTISTIC"

At the time of this heated exchange, I of course did not know any of this. My argument for using person-first language was that I was working with a lot of families who had young kids with a recent diagnosis, and they weren't in a place where they were necessarily fully accepting of their child's diagnosis.

But ultimately I realized that this was an even greater reason to use identity-first language. Our language shapes the way that parents perceive their child. And when we are nervous or scared to talk about autism, that shows the parent that there is something scary to talk about.

In reality, knowing a child's diagnosis is a great thing. It helps us to better understand the child and be better able to support them. And for most families, a diagnosis is a huge relief. It's an answer to years of questions that they have had circling around in their head.

Our language can have an immense impact on families, and when we can show that we are neurodiversity affirming and we are going to support their child in ways that prioritize emotional wellbeing, then we can help parents to see their child through a strengths-based lens. The bottom line is: our language matters.

Side note: Just because the majority of speaking (verbal or other) Autistic individuals prefer identity-first language, this doesn't mean we shouldn't take into consideration the personal preferences of those who don't. It simply means that it's safe to default to identity-first language. If someone prefers person-first language, of course we would use that when we are referring to them.

As I dive deeper into books and blogs written by Autistic people, complete trainings developed by Autistic therapists, and start to consult with Autistic professionals, I start to gain more and more passion for neurodiversity affirming therapy. I bring Autistic lecturers into my online program as well as my clinic, and cultivate friendships with Autistic colleagues. As I started to create my Sensory Certificate Course, it was important to me to make sure that the approach I was teaching was designed to support children's areas of need while also honoring the unique way their brains work.

Am I with Them or Against Them?

One lazy Monday morning I am straightening up the house I was renting with my new partner Chris, who is also an SLP. And let me tell you, with two SLPs under the same roof, both with a love of working with Autistic students, speech therapy is our pillow talk and we're constantly brainstorming how to support kids in neurodiversity affirming ways.

On this particular morning, I am listening to a podcast while our newborn is sleeping and this is my "me" time. It is the first time I'd heard author Alfie Kohn speak, and I was mesmerized by his words. He was being interviewed on *Non-Compliant: The Podcast*, and he was talking about why compliance-based approaches are harmful. After spending so much time with Autistic adults, I was so confused why their opinions weren't being considered in therapy approaches for Autistic kids. If Autistic adults are by and large saying that compliance-based therapy was traumatic for them, why is it still being used? And although I had these thoughts spinning around in my head, it was listening to Alfie Kohn's convictions that made me reflect on how I hadn't spoken out on social media about how I felt. I had been too scared. The world of social media is a frightening place when people disagree with you.

As I am putting a freshly folded pile of nursing tanks on the top of my dusty dark brown dresser, I stop in my tracks. I think about the Autistic friends I'd made online and Autistic colleagues I'd had the pleasure of working with, and how they have been unafraid to speak out against harmful practices, and voice their opinion that therapy for Autistic kids should take into consideration the feelings of Autistic adults. And in that moment, a strong feeling comes over me, maybe my first real life epiphany.

My eyes welled up. *If I'm not with them, I'm against them.*

Silence is complicity. I realize in that very moment that I need to be doing more. And that I can be doing more. I need to take a stand for what is right. I need to put my stake in the ground in saying that these compliance-based approaches are not ok. I need to speak out in support of my Autistic friends, colleagues, and clients. I need to stop being afraid.

It became my mission to amplify Autistic voices. If there are so many therapy approaches that are not supported by the Autistic community, why are they being used on Autistic children? I listened to stories of Autistic friends who were traumatized by the therapy they were subjected to as a child. I knew that we, collectively as a field, could do better. We needed to lift Autistic voices up so that therapy can be designed with their needs and, most importantly, their wellbeing in mind.

Supporting Sensory Needs in Neurodiversity Affirming Ways

One of the most significant ways we can support emotional and physical wellbeing in Autistic individuals is by honoring their sensory differences. Remember that up to 95% of Autistic people have differences in how they process sensory input. That means that the way they experience this world is very different from the way that a neurotypical person experiences the world.

When a neurotypical person goes into a classroom, they can quickly filter out their peer's voices to listen to the teacher. They filter out the distracting visual stimulation—like the carpet with every letter and color under the sun, art projects dangling from the ceiling, pictures of every animal on the wall—and find their desk and sit down. They ignore all of the kids who are bumping into them to get in line to go out for recess.

But for a child with sensory differences, the classroom can be an entirely different experience. The competing sounds of a classroom can be immediately dysregulating. The art on the walls can be so overwhelming that the child has trouble finding their way around the room. The unexpected touching and bumping from peers can be so uncomfortable for them that it causes them to withdraw, or even try to run out of the classroom.

Since Autistic children have differences in their sensory processing, and experience the world differently, that means that we have to honor and accommodate those differences.

Historically, our goal has been to change the child.

The child is sensitive to touch? Give them opportunities to touch a bunch of slimy textures.

The child is sensitive to sound? Put them in a loud classroom for gradually longer periods of time.

The child is sensitive to visual stimulation? Reward them for remaining in a busy classroom.

The problem with this is that we are not moving toward the right goal. The goal should not be to change the child. If our goal is to use neurodiversity affirming practices, that means we are honoring a child's brain differences instead of trying to make them fit the mold of "normal". If the way a person processes sensory input is simply a brain difference, then we should honor and accommodate them rather than try to change them.

Anytime I talk about how I don't support desensitization, someone inevitably says, "Well how do you expect them to survive in the real world?" I also get therapists who say that they work on desensitizing them in respectful ways, or people who say that if a person wants to work on desensitizing to something, they should be able to.

And my opinion is: if an activity is truly enjoyable for the child, then ok. I won't argue not to do it. If a person wants to work on desensitizing themselves to something, go for it. Every person can of course make those decisions for themselves.

But I can't help but think of myself and my own sensory triggers.

When I was filming my course, I had a vision for my outfit. And anyone who knows me will laugh at this because I am about as far from being a fashionista as they come. But I had it in my head that I would wear a navy sweater.

I go on a navy sweater hunt all over Los Angeles. Turns out summer in LA is a pretty good time to shop for a bikini and pretty bad time to score a sweater. Luckily, I find one. There is just one problem: it is cashmere wool. In the past I've never been able to wear wool.

I walk with determination to the fitting room and pray as I poke my arms through the tighter-than-usual-for-a-sweater sleeves. Itchy. Darn.

I buy it anyway. I had been searching and searching, and this was the only one I could find—and at this point the filming is just days away.

As I'm packing for the shoot, I decide to pop a long-sleeved shirt into my bag, just in case I need to wear it under the sweater as a barrier for my sensitive skin.

A couple days later, we're setting up to film. I take a breath of hope while unfolding the sweater. I squeeze it over my head and start putting my hair back in place (I had already done my hair and makeup so I could save the sweater until the very last minute). Approximately two minutes later, I'm back in the room, cursing the overpriced sweater as I'm ripping it off. I'm clearly dysregulated. There is just no way I can do it. I can't be in that dysregulated state while filming or else I won't be in a levelheaded and clear frame of mind. I am relieved I packed my backup long-sleeve tee, and instantly feel better when I put it on.

About 20 minutes into filming, I am at full schvitz, sweating terribly. We are filming in a house with no air conditioning and it is 80 degrees that day. But guess what? I suck it up. I film for six hours in that sweater and long-sleeve shirt and another six hours the next day. Because for me, that is the only option (other than changing clothes of course—but I was stubbornly hanging on to my vision).

This situation shouldn't have surprised me. I've never been able to wear wool. I've spent years buying sweaters that just seemed a little itchy, so I could learn to enjoy them, and then maybe work my way toward wool. But that never happened. They would just sit in my closet, untouched, only feeling the darts from my eyes when I would look at them with disgust, and eventually end up in the donation pile because, needless to say, they did not spark joy.

This is why, when people ask me why I don't work on desensitizing kids, I ask them to think of a sensory experience that they absolutely cannot tolerate, like wool for me. Were they able to successfully "get over" their aversion? I've never met an adult who said yes.

So you might be wondering: if not desensitization, what is the other option?

Enter the word: Accommodate. The most powerful way to support someone's sensory differences is to accommodate them.

Itchy tag? Cut it out.

Too loud? Airpods are amazing.

Too bright? Hat & sunglasses can do wonders.

See how easy that is?!

The beauty of accommodating sensory differences is that it becomes a way of life. And if we can introduce kids to this more comfortable way of life earlier on, wouldn't we want that for them? When children are more comfortable every day, they are going to be able to learn better, engage with others easier, and feel safer.

Win for therapists and teachers.

Win for parents.

Win for kids.

So when I preach the importance of SLPs understanding sensory processing, these are the reasons why.

When we accommodate sensory needs, we establish a foundation of trust with our kids.

When we respect sensory differences, we create meaningful relationships with our kids.

When we utilize sensory strategies, we help bring our kids into a more regulated and ready-to-learn state.

In the following chapters of this book, we'll be diving into the exact strategies and methods I have been utilizing in my clinic, and have taught to tens of thousands of therapists around the globe—strategies and methods that will completely transform the way you work with Autistic kids and the effectiveness of your therapy.

KEY TAKEAWAYS:

» Neurodiversity affirming therapy means we are respecting individuals for who they are. We are seeing their differences, rather than trying to "fix" their deficits.

» The goal of our therapy should not be to desensitize kids, or change the way they process sensory input, unless that is the goal of the client.

» Whenever possible, we should accommodate sensory differences.

Your Next Turn:

Take a moment to journey back to your younger years. Can you remember a time when you were too afraid to be yourself because you wanted to fit in with the crowd? Now that you're older and know more about what you need and what makes you comfortable, can you think of one sensory sensitivity that you have that you don't think will ever change?

Inside Out Sensory Trained Therapist Highlight

If you're working with a child and you're seeing sensory differences, seek to understand them. You can't be an advocate for them when you don't understand their reality, and they can't learn to self-advocate without the validation of their experiences. Seek to understand that person's experience so you can offer support in a certain way. If you see a child completely shut down and quiet, they may look like a good student but they are completely overwhelmed and don't have access to language at that moment. This is how I was as a child - completely silent, stressed; too much going on in my environment to answer questions. I know now, I was completely overwhelmed, overstimulated from the environment around me. Make sure the child feels safe. Make sure the child trusts you. Seek to understand their differences. Try giving them support and see how they participate with that support. Validate them. Give them the words and vocabulary for what they might be experiencing. That will result in them having a better understanding of themself and their differences so that they can ask for the supports they need, when they need them.

Jamie Boyle, MS, CCC-SLP
Autistic SLP & Founder of Speech Baby LLC
@speechbabyllc
To hear Jamie's story, check out Making the Shift for Autistic Kids Episode 7: The Art of Self-Advocacy
https://www.youtube.com/c/SpeechDudeJessieGinsburg

CHAPTER 9

Pedal to the Metal

Bringing Kids into Their Optimal Learning Zone

It's a typical Thursday afternoon and I'm anxiously waiting for three-year-old Autistic Sarah to jet through my therapy room door. We have a waiting room, but no no no, precious Sarah doesn't abide by this policy to wait for her therapist.

From the second she enters our clinic, it's a Sarah chase-down. She goes into as many of the therapists' rooms as she can before she's shooed out, one by one, and eventually stumbles into my office. She runs to my desk to take a sip of my melted ice coffee that I had convinced myself I was going to finish. *Every time*, I think, *when am I going to learn?*

The next part of her routine is to scale my massive black cubed shelves to see if she can grab the kinetic sand, rice, or bean bins before I softly pry her crafty toddler fingers from the top of the shelf. She always seems to be most interested in the activities that will take me three times longer to clean up than it'll take her to play. Fortunately, she's my last client of the day, so more often than not, I have a super fun sensory bin cleaning party by myself while decompressing before heading home.

And I needed the decompression time. Because Sarah was one of those kids who left me exhausted, disheartened, and scratching my head.

She always had so much energy, and I decided that the best way to get her attention would be to out-fun her. I had to be more fun than her and more fun than all of the toys here, and then she'd play with me.

So that's exactly what I did. When she would come in, I would sing hello with as much enthusiasm as I could muster. I would spin her on the swing and hang her upside down. I'd give her tickles and play I'm-gonna-get-you games.

And while she would smile and laugh during these intense sensory activities, she wasn't actually making progress, because I would spend the whole session just trying to keep up with her. And somehow, even with all of the energy I'd put into the sessions, she always seemed to leave just as dysregulated as she came. And to be honest, I would leave dysregulated too.

After one particularly exhausting session, as I am cleaning up the biggest possible mess we could make in a 30-minute session, I ask myself question after question, trying to get to the bottom of why this approach isn't working for her. It's not like I forced her into a cube chair for structured therapy, I was doing the opposite. I was following her lead, just like I was taught. *What am I doing wrong? Why isn't this working? Why isn't she making more progress in her language?* The questions lived in my head rent-free.

As I pull into my driveway that evening, I realize that I had forgotten to turn on the radio. You know when your mind is so busy that you don't even realize you're sitting in complete silence?

That's how I knew these unanswered questions were draining my mental energy.

Week after week, I would lay in bed at night, replaying our sessions over and over, wondering what I could do differently, and knowing that this was exhausting and I couldn't sustain it forever. It was one kid taking up 80% of my brain, occupying 80% of my thoughts. I needed to figure out what else I could do.

I remembered back to my days collaborating with OTs, and that understanding her sensory system would be a big help. As crazy as it sounds, at one point I was actually considering going to school for occupational therapy. I really wanted to better understand those sensory strategies once taught to me by my OT colleague years ago.

I was over the moon when I found out that I was able to get formal sensory training as an SLP. There was a world-renowned sensory program based in Los Angeles, and they accepted a few students each year who did not have an OT background, usually SLPs and physical therapists. I eagerly enrolled and spent over a year taking courses taught by OTs with classmates of OTs.

There was just one problem. The courses weren't designed for me—they were designed for OTs. When I say this, I mean I was writing handwriting goals as part of my assignments. Anyone who is an SLP knows how far out of our wheelhouse that is for us. But more importantly, it was super irrelevant. I was never going to focus on teaching handwriting.

As much time as I spent learning from the courses, I spent an even greater amount of time distilling the information in a way that made sense to me as an SLP, and figuring out how to take the relevant bits and pieces to use in my speech sessions. And although it was a lot of work, research, collaborating, and trialing, it was worth it. I am very grateful that I was able to receive this training, as it helped me realize what components are necessary for SLPs to understand and implement.

One of the concepts I learned was transformational. Not only did it completely change the way I looked at my clients, but when I took it into consideration and made adjustments to my therapy, it had an immediate effect on my clients' ability to engage and communicate.

This is the concept of levels of arousal.

Levels of Arousal

Your level of arousal is the state of alertness or wakefulness that you experience, and this influences how you respond to sensory stimuli. Your level of arousal can be influenced by various factors, such as:

Your environment: When you walk into a library it will likely have a different effect on your level of arousal than when you walk into a thumping club.

Your physiology: We're all wired uniquely—and some people are more likely to demonstrate a high or low level of arousal, e.g., might be more prone to anxiety or depression.

Your health: It's safe to say that when we're not in our best health, our arousal level is absolutely affected. You're probably not feeling like you're going to get your best work done when you're laid low with the flu.

Your sensory differences: The way we process sensory input plays a critical role in how we move through levels of arousal. Sensitive children might take less input to move from one level of arousal to another, whereas less responsive children might take more input to have an effect on their arousal level.

OPTIMAL
AROUSAL

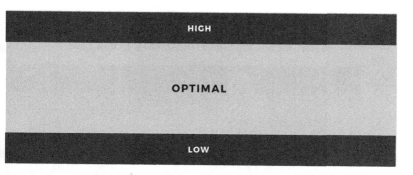

It's normal to move through different levels of arousal throughout the day. A typical day might look something like this:

You wake up with a low level of arousal. You're tired and not fully oriented to what's happening around you.

You start to get up and move and pour yourself a cup of coffee. Eventually you reach your optimal level of arousal (if you're like me, it might take a few cups of coffee, but you get there). When you're in your optimal level of arousal you're able to get your best work done. You're able to think logically. You're able to have important conversations and be creative.

Then, something stressful might happen at work. Maybe it's a coworker causing drama. Maybe a demand from your supervisor. Maybe it's a call from your child's school that they're sick and need to go home. All of a sudden you're in a high level of arousal. You're in survival mode. You're not able to think entirely logically and dispassionately, but you're trying to put a band aid on the situation as quickly as possible.

Then, you take a breath. You start moving toward a solution. And after a little bit of time, you land back into your optimal level of arousal, staying there until the rush of dinner, bath, and bedtime puts your back into a high level of arousal (if you have kids), and then eventually lay back down in your bed, enter a low level of arousal, and drift off to sleep.

WHAT DOES YOUR TYPICAL DAY LOOK LIKE?

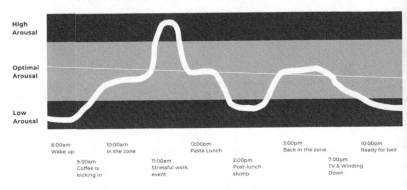

Why were you able to move from a low level of arousal to optimal to high and back to optimal? Because you can self-regulate. You likely know yourself well enough to be able to put routines, strategies, even boundaries in place in order to maintain an optimal level of arousal most of the time. This allows you to be alert in the mornings, do your best work during the day, and fall asleep at night.

But for our Autistic kids, moving from one level of arousal into another can be hard for a couple of reasons.

Autistic kids are more likely to have a baseline level of arousal that is low or high, meaning that they are more likely to "live" in a state of dysregulation, whereas neurotypical people are more likely to remain in an optimal level of arousal or bring themselves back into an optimal state more easily (Tomcheck & Dunn, 2007). Since most Autistic kids have sensory differences, they have to work harder to get into that optimal level. For example, if they have a lot of sensory sensitivities, they're more likely to be in a heightened state of arousal, being on guard for most of the day. Or if they are under-responsive to sensory input, it might take more stimulation than is currently in their environment to bring them from a low level of arousal into a more optimal level.

Another reason it can be hard for Autistic kids to move into an optimal level of arousal is that they may have not developed the ability to self-regulate. So many parents and professionals put such a strong emphasis on a child's ability to self-regulate, but the truth is that it is not even a developmentally appropriate skill for a lot of our young kids. In the first couple years of life, children slowly learn some self-regulation skills such as self-soothing. By age 6, children are starting to get better at controlling their impulses, but their self-regulation skills are definitely still developing. From ages 6–12, children are refining their skills, but our ability to self-regulate actually continues through adulthood. Even as adults, we sometimes wish we handled something better, wish we took a minute to cool off before speaking, or had asked someone's opinion before taking an action. We are all still learning ways to control our actions and emotions.

Self-regulation is not something that just pops up one day, and says, "I'm here!" And it is certainly not something that we are born with. Self-regulation is developed over time through interactions with caregivers who are attuned to our needs (Delahooke, 2019). The best way to teach self-regulation is through co-regulation, which is regulating with the child, being the calm to their storm.

So while neurotypical children and adults may be able to self-regulate and remain in an optimal level of arousal for most of the day, this could be a skill that takes more time in Autistic kids.

Why does it matter? Why do we want our kids to be at an optimal level of arousal during our speech sessions? This is where one of the concepts I learned in my sensory training changed everything for me.

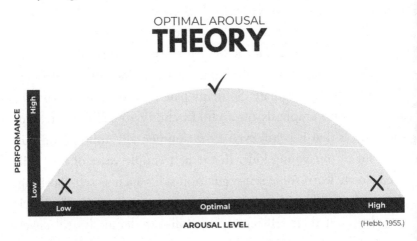

This graph shows that when people have a low level of arousal, they demonstrate a low level of performance. When people have a high level of arousal, they demonstrate a low level of performance. It is only when people have an optimal level of arousal that they demonstrate a high level of performance (Hebb, 1955).

When I first learned this, the concept was glossed over in about 20 seconds during a lecture one day, but I could not get it out of my head. My mind was blown. *So you're telling me…that the reason my kids are not demonstrating a high level of performance is because they're not at their optimal level of arousal?* This made so much sense. It was the exact research I needed to support the idea that SLPs had to focus on regulation for their sessions to be more successful.

I immediately thought about little Sarah. It was clear that during our sessions she was not at her optimal level of arousal. She was constantly in a high level of arousal, and definitely had low performance. No wonder we were not making progress toward her goals.

So now that I knew my clients needed to be at an optimal level of arousal to have successful sessions, the next goal was to figure out how I was going to achieve this balanced state of regulation. How was I going to help my kids reach their optimal level of arousal?

But guess what? After a lot of time and energy that went into learning and researching, collaborating and consulting, trialing and testing, I figured it out.

Steps to Achieving Optimal Arousal

Step 1: The first step to achieving an optimal level of arousal is being able to identify which state of arousal a child is in during your session. If the child is dysregulated, you need to pinpoint if they are in a low or high level of arousal.

What does each level of arousal look like? I'm going to invite our beloved friends from Winnie the Pooh to demonstrate this concept (Milne, 1926).

High Level of Arousal: Think Tigger.

A child with a high level of arousal is likely to appear to have a high level of energy, quickly moving throughout the room. This was Sarah. After a session with this type of kid, you can skip your evening trip to the gym because you just got a full body workout trying to keep up with them.

Low Level of Arousal: Think Eeyore.

A child with a low level of arousal will move more slowly, be more passive, and have less energy. These kids aren't necessarily bumps on a log. Sure, I've had some low arousal kids who just sit tight and hang with me. But I've also had plenty of low arousal kids who move around a lot, it's just that their movement seems like more of a wander.

Optimal Level of Arousal: Think Christopher Robin.

A child with an optimal level of arousal is going to be attentive, engaged, and participating. Keep in mind that an optimal level of arousal does not necessarily mean their body is still, but they are in a mental space where they are able to focus and interact. This is where we want our kids to be in therapy sessions, because when we have a regulated child, they are going to be learning much more effectively.

Step 2: Determine the Sensory Input Needed to Achieve Optimal Arousal

The more I learned about levels of arousal, the more I learned I was doing it all wrong.

When little Sarah would come into sessions, I would muster up as much energy as I could in order to be her super fun and enthusiastic play partner. The problem is that she didn't need 30 minutes of all-out Jester Jessie. Did she need some intense sensory experiences in her sessions? Yes, she did need *some*. But what she was missing was the opposite. She needed me to be the calm to her storm.

Let me explain.

Imagine this:

You go to a baseball game and you're sitting with a bunch of your obnoxious friends who are all overly excited for a sport that you only agreed to go watch because you're a fan of the soft pretzels. As you sit there and watch that game, the energy of the crowd starts to rise, and you start to feel that jitter of excitement in the stadium. The game is tied and then the star player from the home team miraculously hits a home run to win the game. All of a sudden you're up on your feet, cheering like a crazy person alongside all of your friends…you forgot that you never even cared in the first place.

Been there, accidentally done that? Me too.

Now imagine this:

You show up to work on Monday morning and you're feeling pretty good. You've accepted that it's Monday and you've got a busy week in front of you. And then in the hallway you bump into Sullen Sally. Sullen Sally is complaining in her most cringing, whiney voice that she is depressed to be back at work. She wishes it was a three-day weekend so she could go home and crawl into bed. Only minutes after talking to Sullen Sally, you're envisioning what it would feel like to be back home, pull your warm covers over you, and let your head fall back into the cozy pillow. You're not feeling as good about being at work anymore. In fact, you're kind of gloomy now yourself.

Why do these all-too-real situations happen? Why do you get excited about a sport that doesn't mean much to you when you're in a packed stadium with a pumped-up crowd? Why do you start feeling inklings of despair just moments after a complaining coworker unloads on you?

The simple answer is: because energy is contagious.

We can't help but take on the energy of the people around us (Hatfield, Cacioppo & Rapson, 1994). One of those reasons is because of specialized brain cells we have called mirror neurons. Research shows that when we observe someone experiencing an emotion, our own mirror neurons may fire, leading us to a shared emotional experience (Gallese, Keysers, & Rizzolatti, 2004). Research also shows that when we're around people who are stressed, our cortisol levels (stress hormone) increase (Lupien, Maheu, Fiocco, & Schramek, 2007). All of the research points to this: we're likely to be subconsciously influenced by the physical and emotional regulation of those around us.

The thing is, while much of the way we're influenced is subconscious, we can be more cognizant of this process and intentional with noticing our regulatory states, so that we can actually use it in our favor...in life, but of course also in therapy.

When Sarah came into my sessions in a high level of arousal, I met her at that level. Her energy was contagious and I quickly fed off of her energy and transformed into this exciting and over-the-top therapist. The problem is that when a high arousal child comes into session and is met with a tall order of energy from their therapist, the child will likely become even more dysregulated. Why? Because energy is contagious. The child comes in with a high level of arousal, then the therapist responds with high energy, which causes the child to increase their arousal level even more, which increases the therapist's arousal level even more...and on it goes.

Then all of a sudden, the session's over and you have two dysregulated people. The child is overstimulated, the therapist is exhausted, and approximately nothing got done. (In the words of Taylor Swift, "Hi, it's me.")

What Sarah needed was not a souped-up next-level version of me, she needed a toned-down Jessie 1.0.

After having this realization, I go into my session with a new and improved plan. I switch from singing hello at the top of my lungs while flinging her upside down, to singing hello softly while giving her a big hug and slowly rocking back and forth. Instead of reflecting her own high energy back to her, I was giving her my low energy. Instead of reacting to her overstimulation, I was sharing my calm. The whole thing is very counterintuitive. It's much easier to be the exciting play partner for the excited child. And there are times for that, yes, because we want to keep our kids motivated and provide them with the sensory input they need to be regulated. But what she needed in that moment was to be brought down from her heightened state of arousal into a more optimal state for the session.

That explains why you're up on your feet cheering about a sport you don't care about. Now what about the opposite? Why does Sullen Sally always seem to suck you into her lifeless, cold vortex of sadness? Because the same concept of contagious energy goes for a person with low arousal.

Victor was a little five-year-old boy we had been seeing in our clinic for a while. He'd walk in slowly, sit in whatever chair his therapist pointed to, and...chill, would be the best word to describe what he would do. He'd just hang out in sessions, seeming super relaxed, especially for a five year old. He participated in games with his therapist unenthusiastically: not in a negative way, he just seemed indifferent. He didn't ever appear to be excited about any particular game. He wasn't a difficult kid by any means. If anything, it all seemed too easy.

His therapist had a very calm demeanor, and although she didn't have kids herself yet, she had a very nurturing presence about her. She'd sing hello with a gentle smile, and bring out different toys he thought he might like.

The tough thing about kids like Victor is that when a child comes with a low level of arousal, you usually respond with a mental *phew*, and start planning your chill sesh with your chill client. I mean, we don't get a lot of these, so when kids come in with calm energy, we melt into their calming energy and it puts us at ease. Why do we do this? Because energy is contagious. But unfortunately, that chill child might have a low level of arousal, which means that he won't be getting much out of the session unless we can bring him into a more optimal level of arousal.

One day his therapist comes to me and asks if I can observe her session with him. She didn't feel like they were making progress. And I'll never forget the magic that happened with my little Eeyore, Victor.

I enter the therapy room, and he is sitting calmly at the table with a very indifferent expression on his face and passive body language. I immediately notice that he has a very low level of arousal.

I sit down in front of him with a big smile and say hello with excitement in my voice. I sing hello to him with high affect, while giving him spaghetti arms (holding his hands and giving his arms a wiggle). It has an immediate effect on him. Suddenly, he is smiling, laughing, and engaged. All it took was sharing a little bit of energy with him to bring him into his optimal level of arousal.

From then on his therapist used various sensory strategies to bring him into an optimal level of arousal, and he progressed quickly from there. (Lots more coming soon on specific strategies you can use.)

Helping children to get into and maintain a regulated state is an art, and one it takes time to learn. In the next chapter we'll discuss how to master it.

KEY TAKEAWAYS:

» A person's level of arousal is the state of alertness or wakefulness that they experience, and this influences how they respond to sensory stimuli.

» Level of arousal can be influenced by various factors including the environment, physiology, health, and sensory differences.

» Individuals can be in a state of low arousal (think Eeyore), high arousal (think Tigger), or optimal arousal (think Christopher Robin).

» The goal of our speech sessions is to bring our children into their optimal level of arousal, which is the best state for learning.

Your Next Turn:

Think about a past session where a child came in with a lot of energy, and you naturally fed off of that energy. Did you feel that it was the most productive session that it could be? Are you realizing that you might do that often? Now think about a time when a child came into a session with low energy. Did you breathe a sigh of relief and have a "chill" session? Do you feel that child was getting the most out of that speech session?

Inside Out Sensory Trained Therapist Highlight

The great thing about this course is that it's changed my life. And it's changed not only my life but it's changed my practice. Because we all inevitably have those kids we want to reach, but we're not connecting with them. Inside Out has taught me to look at kids in a completely different way. So now as a therapist I have teachers and administration pulling me in, "We have no idea what they need. But you need to see them because you will know." I had an OT the other day say, "I'm sorry what course did you take? Because of your understanding of sensory processing...I've never seen another SLP have that."

Jessica Peramo, M.Ed, MS, CCC-SLP
Founder of Step Up Learning LLC
@msjessicaisback

CHAPTER 10

Slamming on the Brakes

How to Be Proactive with Regulation

Bringing kids into a regulated state is the perfect blend of art and science. The science is thinking about the neurology behind it—how the brain notices and responds to our environment and the people around us. The art is knowing exactly when and how to support each child and their family, while simultaneously working toward improving communication.

Our goal as SLPs is to stabilize the bottom step of the staircase (regulation) as quickly as possible, so that we can move to the next step, which is focusing on engagement. When we can get our clients both regulated and engaged, this is where the learning happens.

In my first year of opening my clinic I read the famous business book, The One Thing.

In it, author Gary Keller poses the question to the reader: *What single action can you take to simplify all your tasks, or even eliminate the need to do them?* Answering this question was tremendously helpful for knowing where to focus my attention in my business.

But years later, as I'm teaching these concepts to therapists to support them in building language in their Autistic clients, I realized how well this concept transferred over to clinical work.

In therapy, you have a lot of goals. You want your client to be regulated. You want them to be engaged and participating. You want them to be motivated by the therapy activities. You want them to communicate. You want them to learn abstract thinking skills. You want them to learn how to self-advocate. You want them to build relationships with peers. To name just a handful.

So if you have all of those goals for your client, then ask yourself: *What single action can you take to simplify all your tasks, or even eliminate the need to do them?*

I found, over years of working with kids, that the answer was: support regulation. When you support regulation, you make every other goal easier, or even render it unnecessary. When your kids are regulated, the learning comes so much more naturally. It's less work for you *and* it's more effective for your client.

If SLPs start with language, they're going to make their job harder. Progress will be slower. Regulation needs to come first. And once you decide that regulation is going to be your one thing, and you put your energy and focus there, then everything else will be easier, or even unnecessary.

The problem is, when you're in a session with a laundry list of goals, a dysregulated client, and a parent questioning your approach, it can feel really hard to justify why you're not directly working on language at that moment...unless you have the reasoning for it. So let's give them a reason.

SENSORY
SEESAW

REGULATED CHILD

Seesaw is balanced.
Child is in his/her **optimal learning zone.**

DYSREGULATED CHILD

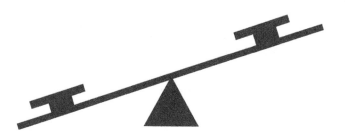

Seesaw is tipped.
Child is **not** in his/her **optimal learning zone.**
Goal is to bring the child back to his optimal learning zone.

It is only five minutes into my 9:00am session and sweet three-year old Ellie is in a puddle of tears on the carpet of my office, her mom sitting next to her, speaking to her with that *You better shape up or ship out because I'm paying for this* tone. Mom strongly believed that in speech therapy we needed to be working on speech.

Moments before, I had taken out my small parachute, and coached Mom in how we could turn it into a swing. We laid the colorful parachute on the ground, Mom gently placed Ellie in the middle, we counted to three and modeled "Go!" We lifted her up and slowly started to swing her as we sang *Row, Row, Row Your Boat*. Initially Ellie looked confused, then her confusion turned to concern, and then her concern turned into sheer terror and wailing. This all unfolded in about 15 seconds.

Now that therapy activity was over. And Mom was ready for the next language building activity. But Ellie was not. As Ellie was crying, Mom was peppering her with questions about what she wanted to do next.

I had only just met this family a couple of weeks ago and we were still going through my parent training materials. But this situation was not a one-off. Ellie had some sensory sensitivities that made her more likely to move into a state of dysregulation during our sessions.

During these periods of dysregulation, Mom would try to coerce her back into the activity as quickly as possible, and usually asked her lots of questions.

The problem was that Ellie was dysregulated. And when kids are dysregulated, placing more demands on them, like questions, will only further dysregulate them. I hadn't taught her mom this concept yet, but as her mom sat there asking her question after question, I knew it was time.

I ask Mom what usually calms Ellie down when she is upset. Her mom says that she likes big hugs while she whispers to her that it's going to be ok. I encourage her to do that now.

After about thirty seconds of being comforted, Ellie has calmed down and is ready to move on. I could have given Mom my spiel about why it wasn't going to help to ask Ellie questions when she was crying right in that moment, but I didn't want to. Usually, I like to bring these concepts up to families before they happen, not after. I don't like for something to happen, and then point fingers, effectively saying, *Hey you know that thing you did just now? That was wrong and here's why.* Instead, I like to save those conversations for the next session, so that we can address it before it happens again.

The following session, after we sing hello, I tell Mom that we are going to talk about how to support her when she's dysregulated. I grab a piece of paper from my desk and draw a schematic of a seesaw: a long line with a little triangle beneath it in the middle.

I say, "Picture a child's regulation as a seesaw. A balanced see-saw represents a regulated child. When a seesaw is balanced, and the child is regulated, this is what I call the Optimal Learning Zone. This is the place that our brains and bodies need to be in in order to process, communicate and learn in the most effective way possible.

"A tipped seesaw represents a dysregulated child. A dysregulated child is not in their Optimal Learning Zone. They cannot communicate and learn effectively when their brain and body are in this place.

"So often, we can tell the child's seesaw is starting to tip, or their seesaw is already tipped. And what do we usually do in those moments? Most of us would carry on with whatever we were doing. If we're SLPs in a speech session, we'll continue targeting our goals, giving directions, asking WH-questions. If we're teachers, we'll continue with the lesson, and continue placing demands on the child. If we're parents, we'll keep going with the activity we were doing. And that's where the problem lies.

"When a child's seesaw is starting to tip, or tipped all the way, our number one priority should be to decrease all demands and focus on getting the child regulated; bringing the child's seesaw back to center. Why? Because when the child's seesaw is balanced, then they are in their Optimal Learning Zone, and it is only then that the child will be communicating and processing in the most efficient way possible. It's only when they're regulated that they can access their upstairs brain."

As Ellie's mom is quietly listening, I'm wondering how much of this idea she will be taking and implementing into their day-to-day life.

Later that session, Ellie became dysregulated after playing with a loud toy. I had Mom reflect back to the seesaw analogy and asked what she thought we should do. Mom comforted Ellie, bringing her seesaw back to center, and we were able to continue playing.

As therapists, the pressure to work on language all the time can make therapy difficult for us. And when we have a parent sitting in on our session, expecting us to work on language, it can be hard to find the words to describe why you need to take some time to bring a child into a regulated state. This is where the seesaw will completely change your sessions. Not only are you able to explain why, at that moment, we need to stop placing demands and instead focus on regulation, but you can teach parents, teachers, and others to identify when a child's seesaw is tipped and strategies for bringing the seesaw back to center.

Being Proactive with Sensory Needs

Another big preventable problem I see, time and time again, is that we let our kids' seesaws tip. We might see signs that it is starting to tip. We can hear it in the child's voice, we can see it in their body language, we can anticipate it by their facial expressions. But again, we continue on with the demands of the current activity.

We need to start being more proactive with regulation and less reactive.

We need to start being more proactive with regulation and less reactive. Right now, in the education field, we're very much in the business of solving the problem of dysregulation. We have a dysregulated child, and because of that their learning is impacted, which means we need to figure out how to bring their seesaw back to center so they're in their Optimal Learning Zone.

But what if we set kids up for success in the first place? What if we did everything in our power to prevent the child's seesaw from tipping? Wouldn't that make a world of difference for the child?

No, not every moment of dysregulation is preventable. And in fact, there are plenty of kids, or plenty of moments of dysregulation with kids, that are triggered so quickly that it can be difficult to help at the first sign; their seesaw seems to tip without warning (or obvious warning, at least).

But there are many, many times that dysregulation can be prevented by being more proactive in meeting the child's needs. And I deeply believe *this* is the problem we should be in the business of solving.

If we know that a child needs a lot of movement to remain regulated at school, then we give them movement breaks during the day.

If we know a child gets dysregulated with the loud music that plays at the mall, we encourage them to wear headphones when they go shopping with Mom.

Professionals often say that this is difficult to implement. It can be hard to meet a child's individual needs when they're in a large classroom. (We'll be talking about setting-specific challenges soon.) But the thing is, when we don't meet their needs, it actually creates a bigger problem.

Say a child is dysregulated in the classroom. Now, the child isn't learning. The teacher has to dedicate time to help the child. It can be distracting for other kids. The child's mental health and wellbeing is negatively impacted in the long run.

But when we can work to meet a child's individual needs proactively, it actually makes life easier for everyone involved. The child remains regulated and is able to learn. The teacher has a clear plan to follow. The child grows up to feel like their needs are being met, which supports their emotional wellbeing.

Being proactive with sensory needs may feel like more work upfront. After all, we do have to know the child's unique needs in order to come up with a plan. But it is much more beneficial for the child in the long run. And it's much more beneficial to those who are supporting that child.

KEY TAKEAWAYS:

» Picture a child's regulation as a seesaw. A balanced seesaw represents a regulated child. When a seesaw is balanced, and the child is regulated, this is what I call the Optimal Learning Zone.

» We need to start being more proactive with regulation and less reactive. We need to understand what makes a child's seesaw tip, so that we can try to come up with preventative solutions.

» When we're proactive in meeting a child's sensory needs, it is beneficial for all involved.

Your Next Turn:

Consider a time when you were with a client and their seesaw tipped.

- What was it that caused the seesaw to tip?
- What was the step you took immediately after their seesaw tipped?
- Has there ever been a time when you have continued with the demands of the activity, even after a child's seesaw tipped?
- How did that affect the session?

Think of one child you work with who has sensory needs. What is one way you can be proactive with meeting those needs?

Want a simple training tool to teach the Sensory Seesaw to others? You can find one in your Ready Set Connect Guidebook.

Don't have the Guidebook yet?

Go to: www.readysetconnectbook.com and you can download it for free.

Inside Out Sensory Trained Therapist Highlight

I'm a school-based SLP, and most of my kids have sensory differences. Some days, my kids would come in completely dysregulated, and I wasn't sure what to do.

Inside Out was the missing piece. This program has helped me to recognize and implement strategies with students based on their individual sensory differences.

I also feel much more capable of educating others about neurodiversity and sensory based therapy approaches.

Chaydee Lawless, MA, CCC-SLP
School-Based SLP

CHAPTER 11

Monitoring the Dashboard

Improving Regulation by Focusing on the Child's Needs

I am walking through the grocery store with my energetic two year old when he flings his arms up, hurls himself to the tiled floor, and begins to scream in good ol' terrible twos fashion. He had just spotted a brightly colored bag of goldfish crackers. "I want goldfish!" he shouted eagerly. And I said the worst word you can possibly say to a toddler: "No…" [Insert that classic slo-mo voice here.]

Without a moment's pause, here we are: his body is spread across the floor of the snack aisle while I am debating whether or not I should scoop him up kicking and screaming, or stand firm on my decision not to buy a new bag.

A glimmer of hope shoots through my mind as I remember I had packed goldfish in the diaper bag that was sitting in the shopping cart. I kneel down to tell him that we already have some. But the crying continues. He is too far gone, as one might describe it: too dysregulated to process the fact that I have a bag of goldfish crackers ready for him.

This scenario was not unfamiliar to me, as a therapist working with young kids. And after I had kids myself, I realized how I could help parents understand this type of situation, one that happens all too often with little ones.

Picture three baskets with eggs in them.

The first basket represents a child's body. The second basket represents the child's emotions. The third basket represents the child's language.

EGGS IN A
BASKET

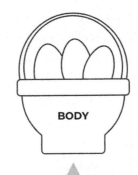

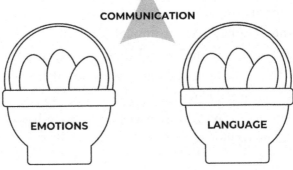

In order for kids to communicate effectively, their eggs have to be evenly distributed among all three baskets. But things inevitably happen throughout the day that cause some eggs to shift into other baskets, which means that more of our focus is directed there.

At that moment in the store, all of my son's eggs went into his Emotions basket. There were no eggs left in his Body basket, meaning he was not thinking about the fact that his body was sprawled face-down on the tiles in the middle of the store.

There were no eggs in his Language basket, meaning he wasn't processing my language that followed the word "No", which was that we didn't need to buy goldfish because we already had some right there in our diaper bag.

At that moment, he was not thinking, *You know what would really embarrass my mom right now? If I threw my body on the ground in the middle of this store and screamed uncontrollably. Then everyone will look and she will totally get me those goldfish.* No, that's not what he was thinking. He was stuck in the downstairs brain and was definitely not conspiring against me.

So often we wonder, *Why aren't they listening to me? Why aren't they doing what I'm telling them to do?*

The next time you find yourself asking that question, I want you to take a minute and think of the eggs in the basket. Where are their eggs? Have their eggs moved into their Emotions or Body basket?

Let's break down the baskets further.

If a child's eggs are in their Emotions basket, they are emotionally dysregulated and not able to access their upstairs brain. Think about if you just found out some horrible news and you were bawling. Then someone from the office comes over and says, *Hey, we're all ordering lunch, what do you want?* Your first reaction is going to be, *WHAT IS WRONG WITH YOU? LOOK AT ME HERE! DOES IT LOOK LIKE I AM IN THE PLACE TO FIGURE OUT MY LUNCH ORDER RIGHT NOW?* Or maybe a nicer version of that. But you get the picture. When your eggs are all in your Emotions basket, you just don't have the brain capacity to be thinking, planning, and problem solving.

Same goes for when eggs are in our Body basket. Now, you can think of a few different activities where a child would need to put all of their eggs into their Body basket. It might be a gross motor activity (like climbing a rock wall, or balancing on a beam), or it could be a fine motor or visual-motor activity (like maneuvering a puzzle piece into a puzzle or stringing a bead on a necklace). I also put sensory into this category. If a child is fully focused on getting a sensory need met with a sensory activity (like spinning around), then their eggs will be in their Body basket.

So next time you wonder why a child isn't "paying attention", try to think about where their eggs are. And remember, it's only when their eggs are evenly distributed in all three baskets that they will be able to communicate in the most effective way possible.

KEY TAKEAWAYS:

» Picture three baskets with eggs in them. The first basket represents a child's body. The second basket represents the child's emotions. The third basket represents the child's language. In order for kids to communicate effectively, their eggs have to be evenly distributed among all three baskets.

» If a child isn't "paying attention", ask yourself where their eggs are. Are they participating in an activity that requires their eggs to be in their Body basket, like jumping or putting a puzzle together? Are their eggs in their Emotions basket, and they are just too emotionally dysregulated to process your language?

Your Next Turn:

Think back to a time when your client had all of their eggs in their Body basket. What were they doing? Was it difficult to target language at that time? Now think about a time when a client had all of their eggs in their Emotions basket. Do you feel they were processing your language at that time and able to communicate effectively?

Inside Out Sensory Trained Therapist Highlight

This sensory training helped me tremendously with equipping me to level up my knowledge and put tools in my pocket that I can use every day: Assessment, interpreting, and implementing sensory strategies based off each individual child's sensory patterns. Understand that even as adults, we can become dysregulated at times. Being able to take that information and look at my own life/body and my own kids and identify areas of need and being able to help them, has made so much of a difference. Not only in my treatment sessions but also my personal life.

Makala Spencer, MS, CCC-SLP
Clinic-Based SLP & Mom of 3
@makspence

PART 3:

Connect

Transformational Approaches to Improve
Regulation and Accelerate Communication

CHAPTER 12

Flooring It

Building Communication Using a Sensory Approach

"Sensory isn't in your scope." I've heard that more times than I can count. I used to get defensive. Maybe because it felt like there was some truth to that, but only because I'd heard for so long that it was part of an occupational therapist's role. It saddens me to think about how many SLPs have avoided learning about sensory processing because they haven't felt like it was in their scope.

There's room for all of us at the sensory table: OTs, PTs, SLPs, early intervention therapists, music therapists, teachers, parents, and Autistic individuals themselves. We all benefit from having sensory knowledge. And when we all have sensory knowledge, the child wins.

We all use sensory to accomplish different goals. The reasons an OT would use sensory strategies are very different from the reasons why an SLP uses sensory strategies.

OT goals are generally fine, gross or visual-motor, handwriting, and activities of daily living (and more), but it's clear that regulation is a crucial precondition for the development of those skills. Just as it is necessary for a child to be regulated to develop communication skills.

As SLPs using sensory strategies, we have two goals: 1) We use sensory strategies to help kids feel more comfortable, safe in their environment, and regulated so that they can better access their language and learn in our sessions, and 2) so that we can take the sensory information and knowledge we have about a child and teach them to self-advocate.

Self-advocacy is an incredibly important goal, and one that is increasingly being added to treatment plans as a result of the neurodiversity movement. Self-advocacy is a skill that we should be addressing from a very early age, and as kids grow and start to learn what their needs are, our sessions are the perfect opportunity for them to practice this skill. After all, SLPs are the communication experts.

Incorporating sensory needs into speech therapy has a massive benefit to both the clinician and the child receiving the services. We don't need to tiptoe around it. Just as with any other type of therapy approach we may use, as long as we are trained, this is something that we not only can be implementing but should be implementing in our sessions. There are a variety of ways that a therapist can meet a child's sensory needs, and we'll be talking about three powerful approaches.

KEY TAKEAWAYS:

» There's room for everyone at the sensory table. When entire teams have sensory knowledge, it benefits everyone, and ultimately, the child wins.

» The reasons that SLPs use sensory strategies are 1) to help kids feel more comfortable, safe in their environment, and regulated so that they can better access their language and learn in our sessions, and 2) so that we can take the sensory information and knowledge we have about a child and teach them to self-advocate.

Your Next Turn:

- Think about your past sessions. Has a sensory-based approach been an intentional piece of your therapy? When you've worked with your clients on their self-advocacy skills, have you ever helped them to advocate for their sensory needs? Do you currently have clients for whom you feel that would be a good addition to their therapy plan?

Inside Out Sensory Trained Therapist Highlight

As a new grad, I was always overwhelmed at the prospect of working with kids who have complex sensory needs. I had no idea what to do and ended up fearing those sessions. The Sensory Course has opened my eyes and changed my practice for good. Not only am I now confident in knowing I'm providing what my kids need, as a recently diagnosed Autistic person, I have learnt more about myself and what I need.

Sam Rowntree, SLP
Autistic Speech-Language Pathologist
@theaussiespeechie

To hear Sam's story, check out Making the Shift for Autistic Kids Episode 16: What You Need to Know About Autistic Special Interests

https://www.youtube.com/c/SpeechDudeJessieGinsburg

CHAPTER 13

Going Full Throttle

Three Powerful Ways to Support a Child's Sensory Needs

slip back into my car after a school observation and melt into the seat, tears welling in my eyes. I had spent the last hour observing my five-year-old Autistic client in her kindergarten class, struggling to participate in the classroom, let alone sit still. Her 1:1 aide sat by her side, velcroing stars to a laminated token board every couple of minutes. "You're working for a break," the aide whispered into her ear after every star.

I felt sick to my stomach as I watched this little one squirm and squeal. The feeling of frustration mixed with sadness and anger bubbled up inside me with every passing minute. It wasn't exactly the time to do it, because the whole class was in the middle of a lesson, but I leaned forward and asked her aide if she had any sensory fidgets she could play with.

The aide quickly snapped that she would get her bin of sensory toys after she got five stars. My heart sank a little further.

When I got back into my car, it was one of the lowest, most defeated feelings I've experienced as a professional. It was a wake-up call that we've still got a long way to go. I had been on the neurodiversity affirming train for so long, was so passionate about what I was doing, and online I was surrounded by people who shared that belief with me. This was vastly different from my online world.

Parked out in front of this school, I felt like a little fish swimming upstream. Surrounded by alligators. I had a pit in my stomach as I thought about all of the systemic and structural changes that needed to take place in educational institutions in order for neurodiversity affirming practices to be accepted. And then I thought about the intense level of training and education that was needed to get professionals up to speed with how to correctly utilize these approaches.

I sigh, knowing it is going to be a long road ahead. And to be honest, at that moment I just didn't know if I had it in me.

But at the same time it felt like I didn't have a choice. Although this was just one child, she was the child in front of me at the moment, the one who would benefit from a change. It wasn't going to be easy, but I committed to taking one step at a time. After all, that's how change happens. Little by little, from the ground up.

I decide my first baby step is going to be educating her team in how to support her sensory needs in the classroom. The trick here is helping the other professionals to understand that this would not just be better for her, but better for them too. It would actually make their job much easier and more successful if we could meet her regulation needs.

At her next team meeting, I explain why regulation tools shouldn't be used as a reward. "It's like giving a child their reading glasses after they finish reading." I go on to explain how sensory materials shouldn't be given to praise a child for completing an activity, they should be used as a tool for accomplishing the activity. Meeting a child's sensory needs helps them to remain attentive and engaged, ultimately having a positive effect on their learning.

Sensory materials shouldn't be given to praise a child for completing an activity, they should be used as a tool for accomplishing the activity.

I talk about the importance of meeting her sensory needs proactively, and introduce three different ways we could support her regulation.

The first way is by using sensory strategies. These would be activities that she could actively engage in to change her regulatory state.

The second way is by modifying the environment. This means changing her surroundings to better support her sensory needs.

The third way is to adjust her routines. This means assessing what her daily schedule looks like and making changes to keep her more regulated throughout the day.

And although it might feel like we have a lot on our plate and so many things to do, it's really nice to have a plan. People like having expectations laid out for them, and steps to follow.

Before we dive into what these three ways to support sensory needs look like, let's jump into what you have to understand first.

Earlier we talked about levels of arousal and the importance of being able to identify if a child has a low, high, or optimal level of arousal. We can influence these states of arousal through sensory input, specifically, input that is either alerting or calming.

It's not necessarily the activity, it's also very much the way we do it.

Although some activities are inherently more alerting (roller coaster) and some more calming (laying in a hammock), oftentimes the activities we choose to do in therapy can actually be calming *or* alerting, depending how we present the activity to the child.

What makes sensory input alerting?

Alerting input is:

- Fast
- Intense
- Novel
- Unpredictable

Imagine stepping on to a roller coaster and fastening your seatbelt. Your heart's racing because you've never been on it before. It starts suddenly and you're off. Up and down, around unpredictable twists and turns. You don't know when you're about to go up, around, or upside down. It slows down in places and then the speed increases without warning. Then it comes to a screeching halt—literally, the screeching of the wheels gives you a startle. You get off the roller coaster feeling energized, hyped up, and ready for more.

It makes sense that being on a roller coaster is an alerting experience. It is fast and intense. The movement and speed are unpredictable. And most of the time, roller coaster rides are pretty novel (unless you've been on the same one 1,000 times).

Let's break down the factors that make input alerting.

Fast: The speed of the input. This might mean that the child is moving quickly (e.g., running or spinning), or that the input is being presented quickly (e.g., child is being tickled).

Intense: When the intensity of the input is increased, a person's level of arousal will increase. Certain activities are inherently more intense than others. For example, rocking back and forth in a rocking chair could be an intense activity if done with speed, but spinning is ultimately going to provide more intense input.

Novel: Anytime we are in a less familiar situation or environment, our arousal level increases. Think about when you get off the airport in a new city and now you have to figure out where to catch your ride. There's an automatic alerting response when we are doing something new.

Unpredictable: Anytime input is presented in an unpredictable way, it becomes more alerting. This might mean swinging a child in an unpredictable pattern, or tickling the child in an unpredictable way. When we don't know what to expect, our arousal level naturally increases.

Now let's talk about what calming input looks like. Calming input is:

- Slow
- Less intense
- Familiar
- Predictable

Now imagine you are laying down in a hammock. There's a soft breeze and the hammock is rocking gently side to side.

It makes sense that laying in a hammock is a calming activity. The movement is gentle, rhythmic, and low intensity.

Now let's break down the factors that make input calming.

Slow: When input is slow, we decrease a person's level of arousal. This could mean swinging slowly, or even singing slowly.

Less Intense: Softer or less intense input will have calming effects on a child. For example, dim lights are less intense than bright lights and therefore are more calming. Certain types of activities will have inherently less intense input than others. For example, sitting on a yoga ball is less intense than bouncing on a yoga ball.

Familiar: When the child is familiar with the input, it will provide more of a calming effect than if it were new to the child. For example, maybe playdough will feel calming because it's a familiar texture, but if a child plays with slime for the first time, it wouldn't necessarily have that same calming effect on them.

TYPES OF
INPUT

Predictable: When input is rhythmic and predictable, it is going to be more calming. This could mean swinging the child in a rhythmic way, or giving them arm squeezes in a predictable pattern.

It's important to understand the difference between calming and alerting input, because it will help you to determine which strategies to use, as well as how to adjust the child's environment and routines to support their regulation needs.

Now that we understand the difference between calming and alerting input, let's talk about the three buckets of sensory-based methods you can

ALERTING

Fast
Intense
Novel
Unpredictable

Slow
Low intensity
Familiar
Predictable

CALMING

implement in order to help your clients reach and maintain a more optimal level of arousal.

Bucket #1: Sensory Strategies

The first bucket is sensory strategies. Generally speaking, these are strategies that a child can actively engage in to change their state of regulation. For example, you might know that when you're feeling unfocused at your desk you need to get up and take a walk. Or when you're feeling overwhelmed, you might take a few deep breaths.

As noted above, self-regulation is a skill that develops over time, through caregivers who are attuned to our needs (Delahooke, 2019). It can therefore take time for children to learn that these are strategies that they can use when they are feeling dysregulated. These strategies may need to be presented by adults to help the child.

Also, some children are more likely to engage in sensory strategies immediately as a method of self-regulation, and some are more likely to take a while before engaging in these activities. This depends on whether the child has active or passive self-regulation (Dunn, 2007). Children with active self-regulation will take immediate action to either seek the input they need or avoid the input that bothers them. Children with passive regulation let input happen to them, and then respond. They might feel that they need a particular type of sensory input, or feel that a specific type of input is bothering them, but they will get to the point where they are overwhelmed before taking action.

Why is it important to know if a child regulates actively or passively? It may be more obvious when a child with active self-regulation is dysregulated, because they're more likely to make a change sooner. For children with passive self-regulation, we need to watch them closely to observe if they are starting to become dysregulated. If we can spot the signs, we can help them to bring their seesaw back to center before it fully tips over.

Sensory strategies can be a powerful tool for changing a child's state of regulation. And since sensory strategies are generally activities that a child actively engages in (at least this is how I typically define them), they are methods that can be taught to kids from a very early age and can be great self-regulation tools for kids to have in their toolbox.

There are endless possibilities of sensory strategies that kids can use. But before we choose a sensory strategy, we want to answer two questions.

1. Does the child need calming or alerting input right now?
2. Which sensory system do we want to focus on?

When a child has a low level of arousal, we can use alerting sensory strategies to bring their level of arousal up into their optimal zone. And the opposite is also true: when a child has a high level of arousal, we can use calming strategies to bring a child's level of arousal down closer to the optimal level.

CHOOSING
INPUT

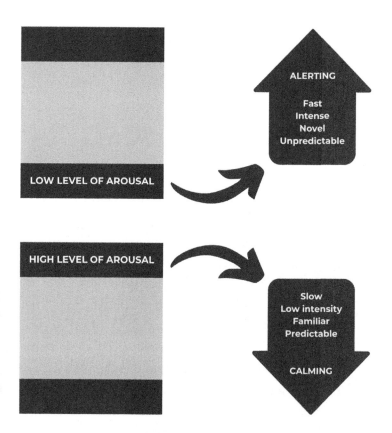

There are calming and alerting sensory strategies for every sensory system. Here are some examples.

Auditory Input

Calming: Listening to soft music, singing softly, white noise
Alerting: Upbeat music, loud music, fun sounds, playing with musical toys

Visual Input
Calming: Dim lights, muted colors
Alerting: Flashing lights, bright colors

Tactile Input
Calming: Playdough, stroking soft textures
Alerting: Slime, tickles

Vestibular Input
Calming: Rocking front to back, swinging slowly
Alerting: Spinning, running

Using Sensory Strategies to Bring a Child into the Optimal Learning Zone

Max and Gio were 11-year-old twins who I reluctantly scheduled to come into my clinic. Any child over the age of eight generally puts me into fight or flight, but we had just hired a new therapist who loved working with older children, so we figured we'd give it a go.

They were non-speaking with limited access to communication devices. They had a lot of needs, and their families were going to require a ton of education and coaching. It was also very clear that our therapists were going to need some major collaboration time with their school teachers and therapists.

The boys came into the clinic, and they were almost completely identical—but their arousal levels were polar opposites. Max was calm, gentle, and slow. Gio was jittery, moved quickly, and had big eyes that were constantly darting around the room.

They needed completely different sensory strategies in order to bring them into more of an optimal state of regulation. Max needed alerting activities and Gio needed calming activities.

We put Eeyore Max on the swing and alternated giving him big pushes and spins as we sang. Tigger Gio sat down on the crash pad feeling the soft prickles of stress ball and fidget toys, while we gave him deep, rhythmic squeezes on his arms and sang to him softly and slowly.

These twins were the perfect example of how important it is for us to choose individualized sensory strategies for each child. It's not a one-size-fits-all method.

Generally, when therapists think about sensory-based approaches, they think about sensory strategies. They think about the activities that children can engage in during a session, whether that's playing with a sensory bin full of sand, rice, or beans, or climbing on gym equipment, or bouncing on a yoga ball. And while sensory strategies are amazing and awesome and transformational for our therapy, there are also two other ways that we can significantly support our clients' regulation needs, which doesn't require much from them: modifying the environment and adjusting their routines.

Bucket #2: Environmental Modifications

It is a Thursday morning and I pull into the parking lot of a nearby gated church preschool. After checking in to the office, I walk into the classroom. It looks exactly like 99% of classrooms in America—like the jolliest unicorn had thrown up a rainbow in there.

The kids are in circle time on a rug displaying every shape, number, and color in existence. The walls are decorated with alphabet cards with animals on them. The children's artwork dangles from the ceiling. The chairs and tables are primary colors, while the reading shelves are pastels. The overhead lights are those long, fluorescent lights with big rectangular covers. The kids get up from circle time and start to move about to get to their centers. They bump into each other as they are navigating their way around the room.

It was no wonder that my little guy who was very sensitive to visual input was immediately dysregulated when he walked into that classroom. It was no wonder that he was a completely different version of himself in this classroom than he was in my embarrassingly organized little office with light gray walls, light covers, and toys stored in black bins each with their own label—not because I didn't know which bin had what toy, but because I felt better about myself as a human when I used my label maker.

The environment we are in can have an immediate effect on our regulation. This is why after 12 hours in Vegas you wish you were going home and you kick yourself for booking a two-night stay—it's just too much stimulation. When you're a sensitive person, you can feel like you've "had enough" real quick, and it doesn't take long for that seesaw of yours to start tipping.

And although sometimes we may feel like we don't always have full control over our kids' environments, or that we can't possibly make significant changes to our environment between every 30-minute session, there are actually some pretty simple things we can do to help.

For one, having a space in the room that is generally less overstimulating. This might be an enclosed area, like a tent, or even just a corner of the room with less stuff. Less colors. Less wall hangings. Dimmer lighting. Even a blank wall in a classroom. These "quiet areas" are great to have for kids who become overstimulated easily, and benefit from having fewer items in their surroundings. This is a great option for classrooms because it is easier to implement a calming corner than having to clear out the entire classroom. If you're in a clinic, you may consider one therapy room being a room that is more of a calming room.

Another rule of thumb: A clean room is a happy room. Even kids who love visual stimulation benefit from organization. Instead of having a ton of open shelves that make your room look like the last standing Toys R Us, either put toys in bins or just hang a curtain over the shelves. You know how they say a cluttered environment gives you a cluttered mind? It's true for kids too. It's always better to have less stuff and more organization.

For kids who need more movement, adding in seating alternatives is a great option. This is an easy way to modify the environment to better support their sensory needs. Maybe that means swapping out a chair for a yoga ball, or putting an inflatable move 'n' sit cushion on their chair, or on the ground under their chair so they can wiggle their feet on it.

For kids who benefit from fidgeting or touch experiences, maybe this means modifying the desk by sticking Velcro across the length of the desk so they can run their fingers across it, or adding fidgets that suction to the desk.

Another powerful way to change the environment is to explore different lighting options. Lights can be off, dimmed, or covered. You can look at floor lamps, table lamps, or lava lamps.

You can find my top sensory toys and recommendations at: www.amazon.com/shop/sensory.slp

Environmental Modifications in the Home

Home can be difficult, and I can speak to that as a parent. It takes about 0.5 seconds to go from a perfectly organized home to complete and utter chaos. A good organizational system helps a lot. Having open bins where you just toss a bunch of homeless toys and missing pieces can get overwhelming quickly. Try getting storage bags for toys that have lots of pieces. Think of every toy having a home. And don't be afraid to donate unused toys! I have a method where I put toys in the garage for a month, and if the kids don't ask for them, then off to the donation center they go. Again, I'm a mom of four, and I know keeping the home perfectly calibrated at all times might not all seem realistic. We're always going to have piles of miscellaneous junk. But the better the system we have, the less clutter we have, and the more regulated the entire family will be. And that's my number one reason for at least trying.

Now that we've talked about all of the different ways you can modify your environment, let's jump into how you can adjust a child's daily routines to better support their sensory needs.

Bucket #3: Adjustments to Routines

I am on a virtual coaching session with a mom in the UK, when she breaks down in tears. She says that her daughter Chloe, a sixth grader who is mainstreamed at a public school, can't enjoy her favorite class anymore. That class is art. The problem is that, with her new schedule, art is now sixth period, and the route she needs to take to get there during the passing period beforehand is so hectic, that Chloe is so highly dysregulated by the time she sits down at her desk. Even after arriving in her art class, the kids moving around and talking feels like too much, and it puts her even further over the edge. She won't even participate in the class. She can't participate in the class. It is the one class Chloe looks forward to, one of her deepest passions, and the fact that she is too overwhelmed to participate just kills her mom.

I ask her mom what she thinks is the most dysregulating part of the passing period for Chloe. We talk about Chloe's hypersensitivities to touch and sound, both of which she is bombarded with in this particularly long and narrow hallway that she needs to walk through to reach her art class.

How could this problem be solved? This is the perfect place to adjust Chloe's routine to better suit her unique sensory needs and keep her in a more balanced state of regulation throughout the day.

We quickly came up with a plan. Chloe talked to her teacher about how difficult it was for her to go through that hall to get to her art class, and asked if she could step out of the class just one minute before the bell rang. Her teacher agreed to this. This meant Chloe could pop out of class just 60 seconds before her peers, and jet down the hall in complete silence. She'd go into her art class, take out her noise canceling headphones, and listen to music while the kids settled into their desks. Then, when her art teacher started the lesson, she'd take them off.

The solution here was simple. Unorthodox, but simple. It was an adjustment to her routine. And yes, it involves a very understanding teacher, and yes, in other cases might even need to involve a written accommodation for the child, but it is possible. And this small, one-minute adjustment to Chloe's schedule was the difference between her spending the next 60 minutes in sensory overload, unable to participate in the class, and her excelling in her absolute favorite subject.

Adjusting routines is an approach to meeting sensory needs that we often overlook. We are constantly thinking about how we can help kids who are already dysregulated with sensory strategies, but adjusting a routine involves taking a proactive approach to supporting the child. It means we need to:

- Write down the child's daily schedule,
- Identify the parts of the day that are the most dysregulating or uncomfortable for the child,

- Figure out exactly what the child's needs are in those moments, and then
- Determine how we can make tweaks to their schedule to help them better maintain a balanced state of regulation.

Another mom I was coaching virtually had a three-year-old daughter named Charlotte. Charlotte had anxiety about going to preschool every morning, so Mom decided that she needed to distract her the whole car ride. Mom found that the best distraction was playing Charlotte's favorite music, and Mom would excitedly belt it out and sing along.

The problem was that, although this helped to distract Charlotte, it was actually really dysregulating for her. By the time they arrived at the school, Charlotte would be very overstimulated, which did not make the transitions any easier.

After a conversation about how we could better meet Charlotte's sensory needs, Mom continued to play her favorite songs on the way to school, but she lowered the volume and sang softly. This made a world of difference for Charlotte. The familiar music eased her nerves, and the soft singing calmed her. Bonus—it also calmed Mom.

By the time they would get to the preschool, Mom was much more well-regulated and was able to co-regulate with Charlotte. She would validate her, tell her how much she loved her, and Charlotte would walk into the preschool.

Small change of routine. Big difference.

Charlie was the four-year-old son of another UK-based Mom I was working with virtually. He needed a lot of movement in order to stay regulated throughout the day.

The beginning of his morning at school was hard because the kids were expected to go into 30 minutes of circle time. But Charlie's little body was craving movement, and he wasn't regulated enough to be able to sit in one spot for all of the morning activities.

I asked Mom what Charlie's morning routine looked like, and it was pretty standard. Get him up, get him dressed, get him fed, and get him out the door. We chatted about how we could incorporate more movement into his mornings, without having to get him up early to get out to the park or something really time-consuming.

I instructed Mom to try turning his dressing routine into a scavenger hunt, and that's exactly what she did. She would put his shirt on the bed, then put his pants across the room, then put his socks at the bottom of the stairs, and his shoes at the top of the stairs. She'd change the locations every day. And by the time Charlie was dressed each morning, he'd already gotten a bunch of intense movement, which set him up for success in the classroom morning routine. Charlie's mom came back and said it was a complete game changer. It was a small adjustment to his routine that made a big difference for him.

KEY TAKEAWAYS:

» We can support children's sensory needs in three ways: using sensory strategies, modifying the environment, and adjusting their routines.

» When children have a high level of arousal, we can use calming input to bring them back to their optimal level of arousal. When children have a low level of arousal, we can use alerting strategies to bring them into an optimal level of arousal.

» We can modify a child's environment to better support their regulation, whether it's in therapy, at school, or at home.

» Even small adjustments to everyday routines can make a big difference in a child's regulation.

Your Next Turn:

Think of one of your current clients. What is one sensory strategy that you feel would help bring this child into a more optimal level of arousal? What is one way you could modify the environment to better meet their sensory needs? What is an adjustment that you could make to one of their routines to support their regulation?

Inside Out Sensory Trained Therapist Highlight

I think the most important thing is just validating an Autistic person and recognizing that what they're experiencing is real. I believe that those of us who are Autistic are just always trying our best, and it often feels like we're coming up short. So giving that validation is just super, super helpful. Being seen and heard, and having our stories listened to can be really important. Especially when you don't know other Autistics in the world, it can feel so lonely. So having someone who validates that is super helpful in our emotional wellbeing, and trusting ourselves and our experiences are real.

Chloe Estelle, Autistic Coach
Co-Founder of OurTism & Inside Out Program Mentor
@chloeestellinyellow
To hear Chloe's story, check out Making the Shift for Autistic Kids Episode 8: Validating the Autistic Experience
https://www.youtube.com/c/SpeechDudeJessieGinsburg

CHAPTER 14

Setting Cruise Control

Sensory and Communication Success in Every Setting

f I had a nickel for every time someone said, "This sounds great but it won't work for me because…" I'd be sitting on a yacht right now instead of at a coffee shop writing this book.

There will always be barriers to implementing a sensory-based approach. That's part of the fun. You have to figure out how to make it work for you and your clients. There are inherent challenges in every setting. And setting-specific barriers are the most common ones I see.

- I can't do this because my therapy room is a literal closet…
- I can't do this because I don't have a sensory gym…
- I can't do this because I do therapy in homes…

That's why I wanted to bring you some inspiration in the form of therapists who have had wild success implementing a sensory-based approach in different settings. In this chapter, you'll meet three of my favorite people, each with a unique background and experience in different work settings, and they will be sharing their best advice about how you can start using this approach, no matter what setting you're in

You'll be meeting Celina, a clinic-based SLPA of 15 years; Melanie, a home-based SLP of 10 years; and Chris, a school-based SLP of 20 years.

Sensory-Based Sessions in a Clinic Setting

When Celina's oldest son was diagnosed with cerebral palsy and seizure disorder, she was introduced to the field of speech-language pathology. After getting her SLPA license, she started working in a clinic, where she remained as one of the team leads for almost 15 years before making the shift to working full-time for me as my chief operating officer of our Inside Out Sensory Programs. She's now the mom of three boys, with her fourth on the way. After having spent years coaching professionals and parents alongside me and our team, she has an immense amount of knowledge to share, specifically for how to successfully implement a sensory-based approach in a clinic setting.

Let's jump into my interview with Celina Wright.

Jessie: What do you think is the biggest benefit to utilizing a sensory-based approach in a clinic setting?

Celina: I think the biggest benefit is the collaboration you have with parents and families. In my sessions, the parents were often right there, helping to lead the session. I think about the parent and child in the center, and the parent is the conduit that leads to everyone else. They are also the constant in the child's life. And in the clinic, you are able to influence this core. Parents can't put us in their backpack. So when we work closely with the family, we can help them learn how to educate others, advocate for the child's sensory needs, and how to set up their environments to be successful outside of therapy.

Jessie: Clinic-based therapists also have a lot of flexibility and control over what we do and how we do it. Could you speak to that?

Celina: First of all, we have flexibility with the design of the session. You can invite parents in for as much or as little time as is best for the child. We can also often determine the length and frequency of sessions. You can choose your goals, depending on the funding source. And ultimately, goals have to match the therapy that we're doing, and if progress is not seen then that is a detriment to the client because funding may be pulled.

Jessie: I'm curious, what do you think are the biggest barriers therapists face when implementing a sensory-based approach in a clinic setting?

Celina: I would say the structure of the environment, which is more of a mindset barrier than anything else. Therapists think their room is too small, or they don't have a gym, or they don't have the equipment, and they feel that prevents them from using a sensory-based approach. That's why I love what we do at Inside Out, because we break down those misconceptions, helping them reframe their thinking and realize that they don't need all of those things.

I also think the physical items can be a barrier. I think speech therapists are initially introduced to sensory as a term, and I often hear "I do sensory"—and what that means is "I have a sensory bin in my office and therefore I do sensory." We sometimes limit ourselves in the actual items that can be used, or we think we can only use specific input, like tactile input for sensory bins.

In reality, there are so many other nuances to the delivery. For example, we can increase or decrease the intensity level of the input. We consider the child's level of arousal. We look at each individual sensory system. And it's exciting when we open people's minds to that.

Jessie: Do you have any advice for the clinic-based therapists who want to collaborate with school-based therapists so they can get on the same page?

Celina: My number one tip is to put front and center that mutual respect, especially for their schedule and time limitations. When trying to get others on board with your approach, it's never helpful to tell someone everything they're doing is wrong and how they can do it better, or overwhelming them with too much information. Sometimes exchange of emails is helpful, but sometimes it's more effective to have a few short phone calls over a period of four to six months. You have to find what works for the other therapist.

Jessie: Any other words of advice for clinic-based therapists?

Celina: This goes for any setting: we have to remind ourselves to continually be in the seat of the learner. Have the parent be your teacher, have the client be your teacher, have the therapist in the other setting be your teacher. Be a sponge to see what they have to offer. We often have so much we want to share and we lead with that. But switching and moving into that seat of, "What do you have to share with me?"—taking on the role of the listener— will take you miles.

Sensory-Based Sessions in a Home Setting

Melanie was an SLP in a private practice working primarily in clinic, home, and teletherapy for almost ten years before moving to work full-time for me and our Inside Out Sensory Programs. She was in the very first cohort of the Sensory Certificate Course.

and when I announced I was hiring, she was one of the first to apply. Melanie's passion for sensory started in her professional work, but quickly expanded while navigating the world of raising her own sensory seeking son. Now she's got her daughter on the way, and with her blend of personal and professional experience, she is the perfect person to share insight into how to integrate sensory strategies into the home setting.

Here's my interview with Melanie Weber.

Jessie: First of all, let's talk about how much you love that drive from home visit to home visit for your own regulation purposes.

Melanie: It's wonderful. I didn't know why I loved it so much until I learned about sensory processing, and I realized that 15-minute break between sessions is absolutely necessary for me.

Jessie: What was it like to be an in-home therapist before you knew anything about sensory?

Melanie: In the beginning of my career I found myself as a new therapist with all of these situations I was not prepared for. I didn't know anything about sensory. I didn't know anything about referring kids to OT. I was often the first provider many of these families ever met and sometimes they didn't even know why I was there. The doctor pushed them to start therapy and now here I was at their house. And being in the home feels very intimate and sensitive. It was very overwhelming at first.

Jessie: What did sensory do for your in-home sessions?

Melanie: Sensory training gave me so much confidence. When you're going into homes, the parents are sitting right there. Everyone is watching you. You don't have control over the environment. You only have what you bring in. And at this time there was a big push to go bagless. The more I learned about sensory, the more I realized that it wasn't sustainable for the parents to have me come in with all of these toys, play with them, and take them away. I needed to explain why I was doing what I was doing, and sensory helped me do that. It's so refreshing to go into a session with nothing but a car key in your pocket.

Jessie: I would love for us to break down some of the barriers to using sensory strategies in the home. We constantly hear therapists say, "But I don't have access to sensory equipment." What kind of advice would you give to therapists who are sitting here thinking, "Well that's true! I don't have a yoga ball. I don't have a trampoline." What would you say to them?

Melanie: No matter what you're using, whether it's a toy or a tool, what you need to know is why that works. The parents are sitting right there and you're saying, "You need the parent to bounce them on the trampoline because..."—you need to know what that "because" is. This means you need to know the input they need and you can explain that to parents. And then you can figure out how to get that input. I might have a talk with some parents, and tell them it's ok for their child to jump on the couch! So for every tool, if you know why that tool works, you can replicate it to get the same input with whatever they have. You can have two adults hold the child in a blanket and create a makeshift swing. Some apartments have playgrounds, and I will go to the playground with them.

Jessie: What are the other benefits you've found to going bagless?

Melanie: Carryover is easier for the family when you use what they have. If you're doing therapy in a sensory gym with a trampoline and a slide, but the parent doesn't have access to a trampoline and a slide, they may not feel like they can do this at home. And it feels like a big unachievable thing. But if you can give them alternatives, it's more approachable for them to be able to understand their child's sensory needs and they don't feel like they have to go buy all of these things to have the same outcome as in therapy.

Jessie: Let's move on to something that still makes therapists uncomfortable, which is parent coaching. My story is probably similar to most. I was parent coaching at 22 years old constantly thinking, who am I to coach these parents? I wasn't even close to having kids of my own. What is important for therapists to know when they are coaching parents in the home?

Melanie: I feel it's so much easier and more natural to do parent coaching in the home. They're more comfortable there. That's their home. That's their stuff. You can ask them questions about what types of sensory activities their child likes. Parents already know a lot about what their child likes, but sometimes they don't understand the connection between what it is and why it works. So if you can name it for them, it gives them so much confidence. In the home, it becomes more a conversation than me teaching and, "You do what I tell you to."

Sensory-Based Sessions in a School Setting

Chris has been a school-based SLP for 20 years. A special education teacher turned SLP, Chris has been one of the thought leaders on the forefront of spreading neurodiversity affirming practices to schools and therapists around the world. A proud ADHDer, he authored the Dynamic Assessment of Social Emotional Learning, which is a neurodiversity affirming assessment for Autistic students. He also created a course that teaches parents and professionals how to write neurodiversity affirming IEPs (Individualized Education Programs), and he just so happens to also be my partner and father of my kids. Having worked in the schools for so many years, mostly with adolescents, and having collaborated with many different types of professionals, he is able to provide excellent input for therapists and professionals who are looking to implement a sensory-based approach in the schools.

Let's dive into my interview with Chris Wenger.

Jessie: In the school, there are so many structures and systems in place, and when you are an SLP trying to implement a sensory-based approach, you can often feel like you're swimming upstream. When a therapist decides they want to start meeting the sensory needs of their students, what is the first thing they can do to get started?

Chris: First and foremost, guide the IEP team members with education and training. This is how you're going to be the most effective. Some questions you can address with the teachers and staff are:

What does it mean to have sensory differences?

How can we support our neurodivergent students?

How can we create sensory friendly environments?

Second, assess the student and the situation. Involve the parents. You have to know the student's individual needs so that you can create environments that are going to meet the child's sensory needs. And when you do that, everybody wins. Administration, teachers, 1:1 aides, therapists. When we can provide sensory supports, we will see that child's true potential.

Jessie: Once therapists are on board and know this is the type of approach they need, the next big question I hear is: how can I build this into the child's IEP? How can we ensure that we're able to use this approach by tying it into the IEP and the students' goals?

Chris: The IEP is meant to help meet the child's needs so they're successful in class and we're prioritizing their wellbeing. There is a Present Levels of Performance page in the IEP, which is a very important page that outlines the child's areas of needs. We can highlight the child's sensory differences in this portion of the IEP. "Johnny does well when provided with movement breaks throughout the day. Johnny gets dysregulated when there are a lot of bright lights or loud sounds around him." Then this document will paint a picture of the child for the team and allow them to create an environment where the student can be successful.

Once you have accurate present levels, you can create IEP goals. Self-advocacy goals are great for connecting a child's sensory needs to their communication skills. Choose a few accommodations that are very meaningful and effective for meeting the student's sensory needs. Johnny's accommodations might be that he can request movement breaks when he feels overwhelmed, or use his noise canceling headphones. Put those accommodations into the IEP and make sure that students know what those accommodations are so that they can advocate for them.

Jessie: Let's talk about collaboration because that's, in my opinion, one of the biggest benefits of being a school-based SLP. You're surrounded by an entire team every day. What are your best tips for collaborating with parents and teams?

Chris: I always keep lines of communication open, especially with parents. I always let them know that they can contact me at any time to let me know about what's going on at home or if they have any suggestions on what could help the student at school. For teachers, I often use quick videos. I explain a concept in just a few minutes and shoot the video over. Part of the collaboration is to know that even if we disagree on the approach, we have to seek to understand. In that case I use a lot of reflective questions to ask for their opinion. I might say, "Johnny seems like he attends really well when he's moving around. What do you think about having him stand in the back of the classroom?"

Jessie: School therapists' rooms are notoriously small, at least we hear that from so many SLPs. We hear about therapists who are stuck in a closet to do therapy. What's your best advice for therapists who have very little space in their therapy room?

Chris: Reduce clutter as much as possible and stick to the 80/20 principle. We use 20% of the therapy games, activities, and sensory tools we own 80% of the time. Store the things you don't need. Make things portable. When there's too much in a room it creates decision fatigue and can be overstimulating. Minimize the items in the room. If you need to create a calming environment, get a light up projector or play some soft music. It's such a myth that you need a big space or gym to accommodate a child's sensory needs. As you always say, "Sensory is not just what you do, it's how you do it."

Jessie: Ok now let's talk about pushing into classrooms. In schools, most therapists are also doing push-in therapy, where they're going into the classroom. And a lot of times they are conducting group sessions. What are your best tips for pushing into the classrooms and for group sessions?

Chris: I always collaborate with the teachers and model what I'm trying to do with them. I show the teacher the sensory activity and then they can see how well the student does when their sensory needs are met. If I walk into a class and everyone is really overstimulated, I'll start off with guided meditation or yoga. If all the students are drowsy and low arousal, I have them choose a song and we put the music on and all get up and dance to get some alerting input. And teachers see how impactful this can be for students.

Students have different sensory needs, and to have effective therapy you have to meet each of their individual needs. I keep a bowl of fidgets that I offer my students—some provide more alerting tactile input, and some provide more calming input. Having different sections of the classroom can help too. Have one area of the classroom that is more calming and quiet, and another part of the classroom is where the child can go for movement opportunities.

It's also important to remember to model acceptance of sensory differences. We all have different needs and that's ok. It's not supposed to be one-size-fits-all. The more you talk about your own needs, the more they will feel it's ok to talk about their own.

Bringing It All Together

You may have been surprised to learn that therapists actually face very similar challenges even when they are in different settings. No matter the setting, therapists have a lot of mindset barriers (for example, thinking that we need a gym to have a sensory-based session), and these mindset barriers can usually be broken down through education and coming to the realization that the picture of what a sensory-based session looks like in their head may actually be very different in real life. We also see that many of our challenges in implementing a sensory-based approach simply stem from not having a clear action plan of what to do and how to do it. This can also be rectified with training and education. As soon as we better understand a child's sensory needs, and feel confident in determining what they need, we can put a clear plan in place.

If you're wondering how to get started, here are two tips you need to know to be successful, no matter what setting you're in.

Tip #1: Remember that sensory is not only what you do, it's also how you do it.

Taking a sensory-based approach does not mean you need a gym, fancy equipment, or even a sensory bin. These expectations about what a sensory-based session looks like often feel unattainable, and stop us from even trying, because we don't believe we have what it takes to start in the first place. If you look at sensory from the perspective of the three buckets of sensory strategies, environmental modifications, and adjustments to routines, you can see that there are many ways to support a child's sensory system that don't involve large spaces or impressive equipment.

While having a gym and all the sensory things is a nice flex, it's really not necessary. What is important is being able to identify the child's state of arousal, and knowing whether or not they need alerting or calming input in order to bring them into their Optimal Learning Zone. Once you have that information, you can determine the ways you will achieve it by thinking about your three buckets, and evaluate your options based on what you have access to.

Tip #2: Collaboration Is Key

Collaboration is an irreplaceable component of therapy, regardless of the setting. In my sensory course, we share with therapists what contributes to success in implementing a sensory-based approach, and one of the key ingredients is collaboration. Of course, this is not surprising to us, as therapists: collaboration improves outcomes, we learn this, we know this. But do we always prioritize this? It's easy to get flooded in the day-to-day and push to the back burner those calls to connect with other therapists, or meetings with teachers, or reviews with families. What if instead of thinking of them as an "extra" part of therapy, or a "nice to have", we think of them as a non-negotiable?

You've probably had families you've worked with where you've thought to yourself, *I'm never going to make progress with this kid unless we can get his parents on board*. We all have to get into the boat and row the same direction. That's not only how progress is made, but also how outcomes are accelerated.

KEY TAKEAWAYS:

» There are mindset barriers in every setting. It's common to think that we need fancy equipment or a big sensory gym to have successful sensory sessions, but in reality, while those may be nice to have, we don't need any of those things.

» Each setting has its own benefits and challenges. It can be hard for clinic therapists to find time to collaborate with outside professionals like their clients' school therapists, but they often have a lot of flexibility over their sessions and may have access to a sensory gym. School therapists may not have access to many tools or an ideal space, or they may not provide many 1:1 sessions, but they have incredible opportunities to collaborate with the school team and are able to give suggestions to help improve their students' regulation in their classrooms. Home therapists don't often bring in outside equipment to use, or get control over what the therapeutic environment is going to be like, but they get to build a strong relationship with families in a setting that's comfortable for them.

Your Next Turn:

Consider your current work setting. What do you feel is the biggest challenge inherent to your work setting? What do you think is your biggest challenge, in general? Is that a mindset barrier, a lack of resources, or something else? What do you feel is the biggest benefit to your current work setting?

Want help working through some of the barriers in your setting? I'll walk you through an exercise in your Ready Set Connect Guidebook.

Don't have the Guidebook yet?

Go to: www.readysetconnectbook.com and you can download it for free.

CHAPTER 15

Taking a Victory Lap

Achieving the Ultimate Goal of Self-Advocacy

I've always said that the purpose of using a sensory-based approach as an SLP is twofold. One reason is to help our clients to become better regulated so that they can optimize the learning experience. The second, perhaps less obvious, reason is so we can teach our kids to advocate for their needs. SLPs are the professionals who specialize in communication, so who better than us to teach children how to advocate for themselves?

When we understand what our clients need, we can help our kids to better understand themselves and teach them how to advocate for themselves. And as much as helicopter parenting may come naturally to some of us, all parents and professionals know that helping a child to be autonomous and independent is one of the greatest gifts we can give them.

Helping a child to be autonomous and independent is one of the greatest gifts we can give them.

I'll never forget a conversation I had with an Autistic colleague and friend, Jamie, who I met after she enrolled in my sensory course. Jamie, like many other Autistic women, was diagnosed late in life. When I was working on filming a training resource, I flew her and her boyfriend out from the East Coast to California so that she could be part of it. Over the few days I got to hear so many stories about her upbringing, and how she came to realize that she was Autistic.

One story that stood out was about how her sensory differences impacted her on a daily basis. She said that, growing up, she would simply endure all of the sensory input coming into her body all day long, then go home and have a meltdown. This would happen every day. For those of you who are unfamiliar with a sensory meltdown, it's a period of time of major dysregulation that can last minutes or hours. For many Autistic individuals, a meltdown completely prevents them from being able to carry out whatever tasks or activities they had planned. Jamie is very sensitive to sensory input, and before she knew about her sensory differences, she dealt with these meltdowns daily.

At 35 years old, as a speech-language pathologist and clinic owner, she enrolled in my online course so that she could better support her Autistic clients. What she didn't expect was that it would change her own life. Through the course she was able to learn sensory strategies, and how to accommodate her sensory needs, which meant coming home at the end of the day and not having a meltdown. How incredible would it be if it didn't take until 35 for most people to get access to that life-changing information?

Learning about your clients' sensory needs is just the beginning. From here, the possibilities are endless. Now you have the priceless, transformational vocation of teaching your clients about how they can help themselves, and what types of accommodations might be best for them. You can educate their families, their teachers, and have these sensory supports written into their IEPs so they don't get washed to the wayside. You can write self-advocacy goals for your clients, which gives you the freedom to target this skill in your sessions. This is just the beginning.

Your Final Turn

I've always believed that our role extends far beyond the walls of the therapy room. While yes, we can make an immediate impact in our clients' lives just in our therapy sessions, our goal for our kids is so much bigger than that. We want our kids to have happy, fulfilling, and meaningful lives. After all, we love them! And sometimes we forget they're not our children and we literally consider taking them home. Our brain doesn't shut off at 5pm: we're thinking about our kids at all times (even if we're trying *so* hard to have work–life balance!).

Our role extends far beyond the walls of the therapy room.

When you commit to making something happen, the path will illuminate itself.

So today I ask you, how committed are you to honoring children's sensory needs?

How committed are you to putting regulation first?

How committed are you to learning more about how to support your kids in neurodiversity affirming ways?

If you're all systems go, I invite you to jump into the driver's seat. We're down on the track waiting for you.

Certificate Program

Are you ready to get in the driver's seat and implement everything you've learned in this book with support from Jessie and her team?

The Inside Out Sensory Certificate Course teaches speech-language pathologists how to confidently provide speech therapy that starts with regulation and ends with life-changing communication.

Get everything you need to become a highly trained, go-to therapist with the power to reach optimal regulation and breakthrough to communication.

If you're ready to:

- Amplify the effectiveness of your therapy
- Learn revolutionary sensory techniques tailored to the needs of your clients, and
- Witness the transformation of your clients' progress and overall wellbeing

Then don't miss the opportunity to join the community of passionate SLPs dedicated to mastering sensory processing and communication strategies.

In the Inside Out Sensory Certificate Course, you'll learn our simple approach, which includes:

- Assessing individual sensory needs
- Designing a sensory-based approach to bring your clients into their Optimal Learning Zone
- Building trusting relationships and life-changing communication

Sign up and, in just moments, you can start diving into the only certificate course that exists to bring sensory strategies to SLPs in a way that's designed specifically for SLPs.

Visit www.sensoryslp.com to enroll.

Speaking and Media

Jessie Ginsburg, MS, CCC-SLP, is the CEO of Pediatric Therapy Playhouse, a top-rated speech therapy clinic in Los Angeles, and the creator of the trailblazing Inside Out Sensory Certificate Course for SLPs & SLPAs. She is an international speaker, writer, and co-host of *Making the Shift for Autistic Kids*, a weekly live show.

She has been featured as an expert in *Forbes*, Care.com, and *Mother Mag*, and has contributed to *The ASHA Leader* and *The Speech-Language Pathology Casebook*. She has spoken at the largest SLP conferences, including SLP Summit, Speech Retreat, and ASHA.

She lives in Los Angeles with her SLP other half, best known as "Speech Dude", and their four boys.

She is available to speak for conferences, events, and lectures. Jessie's goal is to inspire a new way of thinking about the speech-language pathologist's role in supporting Autistic children, and through her speaking engagements, provides neurodiversity affirming strategies for building regulation, engagement and communication.

Please contact support@sensoryslp.com for speaking requests.

ACKNOWLEDGEMENTS

I would like to acknowledge the following people who have shown me unwavering support since the beginning.

Chris: You continuously inspire me to be a better version of myself. You lead by example and magnetize everyone around you. I thank my lucky stars every day that I have such a supportive partner in work and in life, and that our kids get to have you as a role model.

Dad, My Number One Fan: It was easy to choose this entrepreneurial path after watching you wake up every day, and put your energy into all of your passion projects. I am so grateful for the advice and guidance you have given me every step of the way.

Mom: I couldn't imagine getting here without the support you have given me. You are the most compassionate person on the planet, always putting your children and grandchildren before yourself, and I feel so fortunate that the boys get to spend time with you every single day.

My Team: Thank you to my incredible teams, both Pediatric Therapy Playhouse and Inside Out. You have had a massive positive impact not just on local families, but on families and therapists around the world. Professionals like you, who are dedicated and driven to better the world, are the ones who do...one child at a time.

END NOTES

Chapter 1

Greenspan, S. I., & Wieder, S. (1998). *The child with special needs: Encouraging intellectual and emotional growth*. Addison-Wesley.

Greenspan, S. I., & Wieder, S. (2006). *Engaging autism: Using the Floortime approach to help children relate, communicate, and think*. Da Capo Press.

Gladwell, M. (2008). *Outliers: The story of success*. Little, Brown and Company.

Chapter 2

Adamson, A., O'Hare, A., & Graham, C. (2006). Impairments in Sensory Modulation in Children with Autistic Spectrum Disorder. *The British Journal of Occupational Therapy, 69*(8), 357–364.

Baranek, G., David, F., Poe, M., Stone, W., Watson, L. (2006). Sensory Experiences Questionnaire: discriminating sensory features in young children with autism, developmental delays, and typical development. *Journal of Child Psychology & Psychiatry, 47*(6):591-601.

Leekam, S. R., Nieto, C., Libby, S. J., Wing, L., & Gould, J. (2007). Describing the sensory abnormalities of children and adults with autism. *Journal of Autism and Developmental Disorders, 37*(5), 894-910.

Tomchek, S.D., Little, L.M., Dunn, W. (2015). Sensory pattern contributions to developmental performance in children with autism spectrum disorder. *American Journal of Occupational Therapy, 69*(5): 1-10.

Chapter 3

Kohn, A. (1993). *Punished by rewards: The trouble with gold stars, incentive plans, A's, praise, and other bribes.* Houghton Mifflin.

Lavoie, R. (2007). *The motivation breakthrough: 6 secrets to turning on the tuned-out child.* Simon & Schuster.

Chapter 7

Siegel, D. J., & Bryson, T. P. (2011). *The Whole-Brain Child: 12 Revolutionary Strategies to Nurture Your Child's Developing Mind.* Delacorte Press.

Chapter 9

Tomchek, S. D., & Dunn, W. (2007). Sensory processing in children with and without autism: A comparative study using the short sensory profile. *American Journal of Occupational Therapy, 61*, 190–200.

Delahooke, M. (2019). *Beyond behaviors: Using brain science and compassion to understand and solve children's behavioral challenges.* PESI Publishing & Media.

Hebb, D. O. (1955). Drives and the CNS (conceptual nervous system). *Psychological Review, 62*(4), 243.

Milne, A. A. (1926). *Winnie the Pooh.* Methuen & Co. Ltd.

Hatfield, E., Cacioppo, J. T., & Rapson, R. L. (1994). *Emotional contagion.* Cambridge University Press.

Gallese, V., Keysers, C., & Rizzolatti, G. (2004). A unifying view of the basis of social cognition. *Trends in Cognitive Sciences, 8*(9), 396-403.

Lupien, S. J., Maheu, F., Tu, M., Fiocco, A., & Schramek, T. E. (2007). The effects of stress and stress hormones on human cognition: Implications for the field of brain and cognition. *Brain and Cognition, 65*(3), 209-237.

Chapter 10
Keller, G., & Papasan, J. (2013). *The ONE Thing: The Surprisingly Simple Truth Behind Extraordinary Results.* Bard Press.

Chapter 11
Hayden, D. (2009). The PROMPT model: Use and application for children with mixed phonological-motor impairment. *International Journal of Speech-Language Pathology, 8*, 265-281.

Chapter 13
Delahooke, M. (2019). *Beyond behaviors: Using brain science and compassion to understand and solve children's behavioral challenges.* PESI Publishing & Media.

Dunn, W. (2007). *Sensory Processing Framework.*

ABOUT THE AUTHOR

Jessie Ginsburg

Jessie is a sensory trained speech-language pathologist who has trained
tens of thousands of professionals and
families around the globe in how to
build communication through a sensory-based approach. She is the founder of Pediatric Therapy Playhouse, a
top-rated clinic in Los Angeles, and the
creator of the trailblazing Inside Out
Sensory Certificate Course. Through
her international publications and talks, Jessie inspires a new way
of thinking about the speech-language pathologist's role in supporting Autistic children. She lives in Los Angeles with her SLP
other half, best known as "Speech Dude", and their four boys.

Made in the USA
Las Vegas, NV
16 September 2024

95225174R00095